Dyadic Communication: A Transactional Perspective

Dyadic Communication: A Transactional Perspective

William W. Wilmot
University of Montana

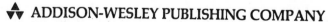 **ADDISON-WESLEY PUBLISHING COMPANY**
Reading, Massachusetts • Menlo Park, California
London • Amsterdam • Don Mills, Ontario • Sydney

This book is in the
ADDISON-WESLEY SERIES IN HUMAN COMMUNICATION

Consulting Editor
C. David Mortensen

ISBN 0-201-08615-8
DEFGHIJ-DO-798

*To my mistress, hiking buddy,
friend, and wife, Charney.
May our dyad continue to prosper.*

Foreword

Society is often described as an ongoing system of communication maintained by persons committed to the principle of consistent action. Similarly, this series in Human Communication is designed to explore the ongoing and pervasive impact of communication on the actions and patterns of everyday experience. The series provides a flexible and integrated discussion of key concepts, problems, topics, and issues related to "person-centered" subject matter. The books strive to be readable, nontechnical, and broadly based without sacrificing the depth needed to challenge serious students.

In developing such an important collection of texts, Addison-Wesley has called upon a well-known group of teachers whose competence is ideally suited to their texts. *Communication Inquiry: A Perspective on a Process* by Gerald R. Miller and Henry E. Nicholson introduces students to various ways of studying communicative behavior as an integral dimension of personal and social experience. *Dyadic Communication: A Transactional Perspective* by William W. Wilmot focuses on the complex and fascinating processes that shape the experience of communication in interpersonal social situations. *Communication and Social Influence* by Stephen W. King broadens the study of communication to the context of what is known about the potentials and hazards of using language to influence and persuade others. An overview of language and speech as communication codes, within and between individuals, is the subject of Larry Wilder's *Speech, Language, and Communication* (forthcoming). The larger theoretical aspects of human communication are examined in *Pragmatics of Analoguing: Theory and Model Construction in Communication* by Leonard C. Hawes and in *Perspectives on*

Communication Theory by Jesse G. Delia (forthcoming). *Pragmatics of Analoguing* provides the first systematic treatment of the requirements of developing theories about the underlying nature of communicative experience. Delia's text will complement other books in the series by providing a broadly based synthesis of recent contributions to the study of communication theory.

These brief, integrated paperback texts are suitable for a wide range of purposes and courses within communication and the social sciences. Used in combination or alone with other texts and supplements, they will enhance and enrich the study of human communication.

C. David Mortensen

Preface

For people interested in human communication, the dyadic or two-person context offers rich opportunities for insight. Within this context, the basic components of the communication system can be identified, the nature of relationships *per se* can be focused upon, and the intricacies of relationships can be charted. And equally important, the mutual effects participants have on each other are easily seen. Basically, the dyadic context allows one to observe the fundamental elements that operate in interpersonal communication relationships.

As this book emerged, it became clear what my major challenge was: to present the transactional view of communication in a meaningful, interesting fashion. Throughout I have tried to strike a balance between developing a coherent perspective toward dyadic communication and presenting provocative illustrations to keep the reader interested. Numerous friends helped me achieve these two goals. Students who read parts or all of the manuscript and supplied valuable comments were Wayne Beach, Wayne Buchanan, John Cote, Bob Geis, Sharon McGuire, Cinda Purdy, and Valori Schultz. The eighteen students of *Interpersonal Communication 599: Dyadic Communication* provided social support for, and intellectual challenge to, many of the ideas contained here. To all of these "unofficial" reviewers, I offer my sincere thanks.

The "fantastic five," the official reviewers supplied through the cooperation of Addison-Wesley's Larry Jones, were truly remarkable. They were Stephen King, David Mortensen, Malcolm Parks, Duane Pettersen, and John Wenburg. This uncompromising bunch did the impossible by simultaneously demanding excellence while bestowing friendship. I am fortunate to have friends who are also scholars.

Michelle Peterson, with typewriter at hand, waded through my poor penmanship and cut-and-paste jobs and produced a beautiful manuscript. For her patience I thank her. My colleagues in the Department of Interpersonal Communication helped by giving support and challenge at crucial places during development of the manuscript.

I have a vague feeling that I have forgotten someone who helped me during this project. Whoever you are, please call or write me so I can thank you.

Two very notable distractions helped me immeasurably. The mountains of Montana and my wife, Charney, banded together as a team to keep me in touch with reality.

Missoula, Montana   Bill Wilmot
January 1975

Contents

PART I   DYADIC ELEMENTS

Chapter 1   The Nature of Dyadic Transactions 1

Dyadic communication defined 6
Dyadic communication is transactional 8
Characteristics of dyads 12
    Intimacy 13
    Completeness 16
    Distinctiveness from larger groups.................... 18
The triad: dyadic in nature 20
    Is a triad possible? 20
    A triad dissected.................................. 22
    Enter the third party 23
    Which dyad will form? 27
Summary 28

Chapter 2   Perception of the Self 31

Components of the self-concept 35
    Degrees of self-awareness 35
    Multiple selves 37
The social self 41
    The looking-glass self 43
    The self by social comparison 47
    Playing social roles 49
Maintenance and change of self-concept 51
Summary 55

Chapter 3   Perception of the Other   57

The transactional nature of person perception   59
Perceptual regularities   62
  Imposing structure   62
  Attributing causality   64
Accuracy in perception   65
Interpersonal attraction   68
  Propinquity   68
  Similarity   71
  Behavior   73
Summary   74

PART II   RELATIONSHIPS: THE KEY TO TRANSACTIONS

Chapter 4   The Nature of Dyadic Relationships   79

I see you seeing me   81
The communication system   82
Relational fundamentals   84
  The coorientation model   84
  The interpersonal perception method   88
The negotiation of social identities   94
Issues and relationships   96
Dimensions of relationships   103
  Dominance/submission   106
  Love/hate   109
Reciprocity: a dyadic norm   110
Summary   113

Chapter 5   Relational Intricacies: Self-Fulfilling Prophecies, Spirals
            Paradoxes, and Do-Loops   115

Self-fulfilling prophecies   117
Spirals   122
  Progressive spirals   124
  Regressive spirals   126
  Alternating spirals   127
Paradoxes   130
Do-loops   135
Summary   139

Chapter 6   Improving Dyadic Relationships 141

Personal improvements 143
   Analyze your needs 144
   Check your perceptions 145
   Confirm the other 150
Relationship improvements 152
   Analyze the relationship 152
   Influencing the direction of the relationship 157
Summary 159

Appendix   Categories of Interpersonal Response 161

References 167

Part I
Dyadic
Elements

Chapter 1
The Nature of
Dyadic
Transactions

. . . much of the social activity of individuals today can be described as search behavior—a relentless process of social discovery in which one seeks out new friends to replace those who are either no longer present or who no longer share the same interests

—Alvin Toffler, *Future Shock*

In our highly mobile society, our relationships with others are continually changing. Whether you leave home to attend college, change jobs, get married (or divorced), or join new groups, your friendship patterns change. As your close friends of yesterday become more of a memory, you replace them with others. It is, in fact, rather unlikely that your best friends of five years ago are the same ones you would mention as being your best friends today.

The degree of changes we experience in our interpersonal relationships can be, from one point of view, cause for concern. It may be that we have entered a "psychological ice age," and that except for "occasional bursts of warmth, often fueled by sex after a few cocktails, truly intimate encounters have begun to disappear from civilized Western life" [13]. Certainly in many of our day-to-day communication transactions, we operate in "reciprocal ignorance" of each other [132]. Do you know anything or care about the lives of the people who sell you groceries, clothes, and gasoline, and do they know anything at all about you? If the people in your life are transitory, why should you attempt to establish any meaningful communication with them?

On the more optimistic side, our degree of autonomy and anonymity can provide benefits. If you are unhappy with your situation, you can often change it. A new job and friends can provide "breathing room" for you to maximize your potential and lead the type of life that suits you. And just because you slide by hundreds or thousands of people daily does not mean that you are incapable of forming meaningful relationships with select people. It may be that our mobility provides us with more acquaintances and fewer friends but the friendships we do have are highly engaging and meaningful. Whatever your position is on this issue, it is clear that communication relationships are a very significant part of our lives. In almost all professions, for instance, "People spend approximately three-fourths of their waking time communicating with others" [252]. Even

3

in highly technical occupations such as research and development, "communication with people, not equipment, is the principal focus of activity" [150]. Communication with others is an inescapable factor of our existence.

This book focuses on dyadic communication, which is defined as two people involved in a face-to-face transaction. Any direct communicative transaction between two people, whether it be fleeting or recurring, is dyadic. Friendship pairs, marital couples, business partners, a parent-child relationship, or two persons having coffee for the first and last time, all constitute dyads. Whether or not the two participants differ in age, sex, color, or any other variable, as long as they are engaging in *face-to-face communication*, they are considered as having a dyadic relationship. Two-person relationships that are outside the realm of face-to-face communication can, of course, occur also [326]. Placing a telephone call to a friend or writing that person a letter are also communicative actions, but such indirect transactions are beyond the scope of this book.

Dyadic relationships occur in numerous contexts. Leopold Von Wiese [320] has provided a sample classification of some dyadic pairs (Fig. 1–1).

Take time to become familiar with Fig. 1–1, because the terminology presented there will be used throughout this book, with one small exception. What Von Wiese labeled as sexual pairs will be referred to as romantic pairs. As you can see from his list, a romantic pair incorporates premarital dating couples, marital pairs, as well as extramarital relationships. Homosexual as well as heterosexual relationships qualify as romantic types of dyads. Notice that what Von Wiese labeled as typical pairs are those that are often thought of as being more personal—romantic, family, and friend relationships. Atypical pairs are usually formed in employment contexts.

In the first major unit of the book, these dyadic types of interpersonal relationships will be used to develop an overview of dyadic communication. The current chapter sets the backdrop for the study of dyadic transactions by defining dyadic communication, illustrating the fundamental characteristics of a transactional point of view, and pinpointing the distinctive features of dyads compared to communicative groups of three or more. The building blocks for an understanding of elements present in all dyadic transactions are presented in Chapters 2 and 3, "Perception of the Self" and "Perception of the Other," respectively.

The second major unit, "Relationships: The Key to Trans-actions," presents an analysis of dyadic communication from a relationship point of view. In fact, the first three chapters comprising Part I set the stage for such a relational analysis. Chapter 4 of Part II

I. TYPICAL (GENUINE) PAIRS
A. Sexual pairs
  1. Heterosexual
     a) Premarital and extramarital
     b) Marital
  2. Homosexual
B. Generation pairs
  1. Father-son group
  2. Father-daughter group
  3. Mother-son group
  4. Mother-daughter group
  5. Parental pair
  6. Sibling pair
  7. More general; adult-child group
C. Friendship pair

II. ATYPICAL (DERIVATIVE) PAIRS
(Only a few of the more important examples of atypical groups can be given here.)
A. Superior-subordinate (frequently but not always in pair relationship)
  1. Professor-assistant
  2. Captain-mate
  3. Physician-nurse
  4. Officer-orderly
  5. Political boss-henchman.
     Etc.
B. Aider-aided
  1. Physician-patient
  2. Supervisor-delinquent
  3. Pastor-parishioner
  4. Attendant-inmate
  5. Social worker-client
     Etc.
C. Teacher-pupil
D. Pairs primarily conditioned by the economic order

1. Master-journeyman	5.	Mistress-maid
2. Master-apprentice	6.	Guide-tourist
3. Foreman-workman	7.	Executive-secretary
4. Engineer-fireman		Etc.

Fig. 1-1 Classification of dyadic groups. (From Leopold Von Wiese, *Systematic Sociology.* New York: Wiley, 1932, p. 509. By permission.)

explains the nature of relationships, detailing some techniques for ob-serving relationships and highlighting some principles common to all dyadic relationships. Chapter 5, "Relational Intricacies: Self-Ful-filling Prophecies, Spirals, Paradoxes, and Do-Loops," is a treatment of some provocative aspects of dyadic communication frequently overlooked. The final chapter, "Improving Dyadic Relationships," contains some specific suggestions that could be helpful in improving the quality of your dyadic relationships.

As is the case with any work, this one rests on some basic assumptions about the nature of man and his communication. Specifically, it assumes that:

1. we act toward ourselves, other people, and objects based on the meanings they have for us, and

2. the meanings we acquire are derived from our communicative transactions with others.*

The heart of dyadic and, in fact, all interpersonal communication lies in the meanings we acquire in our transactions with our environment.

DYADIC COMMUNICATION DEFINED

Just what is this process called communication? The word "communication" is bandied about (and claimed as their own property) by public speakers, advertisers, specialists in audiovisual aids, human-relations trainers, and even college professors. To some people, communication occurs when a TV station sends signals from its tower; for others "real" communication occurs only when two people reach perfect understanding. Within the dyadic context, or any face-to-face group, communication occurs when a person *assigns meaning* to the behavior of another.

As an outsider looking in, it is difficult to specify when a participant in a transaction has assigned meaning to the behavior of another. But when you are in a dyad as a participant, you are aware when you do. When you take cognizance of the other person and react, you have assigned meaning. For example, consider two young college girls "studying" together. When their eyes meet and girl *A* makes a face, girl *B* assigns meaning to it and she breaks out laughing. Clearly, both girls are assigning meaning to the other's behavior.

---

*These assumptions parallel closely, in expanded form, those made by the symbolic interactionist school of thought. See Blumer [34].

Lest you be misled, one partner in a dyad does not have to consciously send a "message" to the other. If girl *A* had been daydreaming when girl *B* looked at her, communication still would have occurred. Whatever girl *A* does or does not do in the presence of girl *B* potentially has meaning for girl *B*. Put bluntly, when you are in the presence of another, *you cannot not communicate* [330]. Everything you do, or do not do, may have meaning for the other person. Take the case of two young men having a coke together. One man says, "Hey, Charley, I've just been put on a retainer for a life insurance company and it will be a fantastic opportunity to pick up some much needed money." Charley just sits there, thinking to himself what a greedy fellow his friend is. The first man tries again. "Charley, this is really a lucky break, isn't it?" And Charley just sits there. Is Charley communicating to the first man? He certainly is! He is shouting loud and clear, without making a sound, that he is not interested.

The assignment of meaning to someone's behavior is not an objective, fixed event. It happens within people's heads; it is a personal process [334]. No matter what you do or say, you *do not* control the impressions others may have of you. You may react to your own behavior and see yourself as poised, deliberate, and ladylike (or manlike). But other people may see you as aloof and distant. *Each* person assigns his *own* meaning to your behavior; it may or may not be similar to yours or to other people's assessments.

In a two-person context, it sometimes happens that the participants are not mutually aware of each other. If only one person assigns meaning to the other's behavior, communication has occurred. For example, take two people *A* and *B*. When *A* perceives *B* (even if *B* doesn't see him), communication has occurred. Likewise when *B* sees *A*, communication has occurred. But until *A* sees *B* seeing him (and, of course, *B* sees *A* seeing him), the *dyad has not functioned as a unit*. We have to think of the two together, rather than separately [160]. Put another way, the dyad begins to function when there is the "possibility that the actions of each person affect the other" [307]. There is potential mutual influence. If *A* is watching *B*, but *B* does not see *A*, then the actions of *A* cannot influence *B*. Rambunctious grade-school students use this principle as the guide for when to stick out their tongues at the teacher. Aside from those teachers who have eyes in the back of their heads, if the teacher cannot perceive their behavior, they escape being sent to the principal's office. A dyad begins to function as a unit, then, when there is the "perception of being perceived." When you as a participant in a dyad are aware that the other person sees you, the relationship has been formed. Each person sees the other seeing them.*

An awareness of when a relationship is created is not only instructive, it can be fun. For someone who wants to watch you and *not* enter into a relationship, your recognition of them can be embarrassing. The next time you are stopped at a traffic light in your car and the person in the car next to you is staring at you, just turn, face them, give a friendly smile and wave. You are saying, "Aha! I see you seeing me!" They quickly turn away and pretend that they were not seeing you. (But they saw you seeing them see you, and they are trapped! Your response to them created a relationship which they did not want to occur.)

DYADIC COMMUNICATION IS TRANSACTIONAL

Communication is defined as the process of assigning meaning. Each perception we make of our environment is a transactional process between us and the object(s) we perceive. What we see "out there" is just as much a function of us as it is of the object(s). A simple illustration should suffice. When the author and his wife moved to Montana, we both felt a great sense of relief. Here at last was a place where we felt free. As we gaze at mountains, they seem to open up the world for us. Last year a couple moved next door who had lived in the same midwestern city as we had. One day while standing on our front lawn, we had a discussion about mountains. To them, having experienced the mountains less often than we, the towering peaks were confining. In fact, the lady told us that she wanted to leave town to "get out of prison." We look at the same mountains, from the same spot, and see opposite things. Stated another way, each individual's reality is a process of his assumptions [223]. In short, the entire perceptual process is a transaction between the person and the object perceived. The entire process of living "is a constant flow of transactions in which an individual participates and from which he derives all his experience" [50].

---

*Chapter 4, "The Nature of Relationships," deals with this situation in considerable detail

The process of human communication has an added element that renders it decidedly transactional. Our perceptions of people, as with objects, are filtered through our interpretations. But in addition, our perception of another and our subsequent behavior can actually change the behavior of the person we see.* Your own behavior affects the behavior of others around you; they are behaving within a particular context and so are you. Put more simply, communication is *contextual.* You behave differently around your parents than you do around your romantic partner. And each of them behaves differently in other contexts. Each person in a dyadic transaction is affected by the presence of the other.

Because each participant is affected in a dyadic transaction, dyadic communication is *not* a linear, one-way event. You do not communicate *to* someone as if they were an inert blob of clay; you communicate *with* another. You do not originate communication; you participate in it [330]. Some people erroneously think that communication is a tool, something to be turned off and on at will, to be used or not. Such a view is shortsighted. If, for example, you are a salesman and your task is to sell a product, it is easiest to see yourself communicating to someone. You are giving the message and the client is absorbing it. You are the "seller" and he is the "sellee." This point of view ignores two important points: (1) One cannot *not* communicate (*both* of you are attaching meaning to the transaction), and (2) when you create a message it affects you, too. One cannot create a message without it affecting himself. The process of your creating a message may affect you *more than* it does the person receiving it. Your participation in an encounter means that it will affect you, whether you are primarily creating or primarily deciphering the verbal message.

A recent experiment with behavioral modification vividly demonstrates the joint effects present in a communicative transaction [109]. In Visalia, California, students who had behavior problems were placed in a special class for "incorrigibles." In this particular instance, the students were given training in behavior modification. When they returned to their regular classes, unknown to the regular teacher, they engaged in a systematic attempt at behavior modifi-

---

*Chapter 5 deals specifically with this process under the label of self-fulfilling prophecies

cation. The goal was simple—to encourage positive teacher behavior toward themselves. Some students had such long histories of receiving only negative teacher behavior that they could not identify positive behavior when it occurred. After training with videotapes and role playing, they had become skilled in identifying positive teacher behavior. The students systematically praised and encouraged the teachers whenever the teacher gave them a positive response. The results were fascinating. The teachers' behavior changed dramatically; they became more positive. And the student behavioral engineers began enjoying school and performing more successfully.

From a transactional point of view, the crucial question is, Who changed whom? The students thought the teachers changed and the teachers "tended to think of the projects as having changed the children rather than themselves" [109]. The transactional point of view stresses that to accurately describe communication, we need to think of people together rather than think of each person separately [160]. Their relations are interpenetrative; *each person influences and is influenced by the other* [315].

Since the process of dyadic communication is transactional, some of the terminology applied to communication is inaccurate. For instance, numerous writers on communication refer to "senders" and "receivers." But in any dyadic transaction each participant is simultaneously sending and receiving [334]. For instance, when you are engaged in conversation with someone, while you are creating cues (talking, sitting erect) you are attaching meaning to the cues sent by the other (he is looking at you and twirling a pencil). Likewise in that same frame of time, the other person is both sending and receiving cues. You are both participating, and in this book the term "participant" is used in place of "sender" and "receiver."

A related point must also be made. A transactional event cannot be adequately characterized from the action-reaction perspective. A pool game, in which the cue ball is the action (stimulus) and the eight ball in the corner pocket is the reaction (response), can be adequately viewed from the action-reaction perspective. But human beings are not billard balls. The analysis of a pool game is not sufficient to describe a communicative process. But obviously it may be useful for purposes of partial description to label some elements of a transaction as causes or stimuli (independent variables) and others as effects or responses (dependent variables). For example, if a young man is attractive, then a person meeting him may respond favorably to his attractiveness. We can label the "attractiveness" as the independent variable to see what behavioral effects it produces. If we do, we have specified an independent variable (attractiveness) and a dependent variable (the responses to attractiveness). Our distinction may be instructive because we can conclude that attractiveness produces such-and-such effects. The important point to note, however, is that we could just as easily have specified attractiveness as a dependent variable. If we did, then we would be concerned with questions like, What produces perceived attractiveness? Regardless of what we select as the independent and dependent variables in a communication transaction, we have made an *artificial distinction*. In any communication situation, any variable can be seen as independent *or* dependent, contingent on your point of view.* But whatever choice you make, the distinction is a function of you rather than of the communication situation. The communication situation is more complex than the listing of independent and dependent variables would make it appear. There is a "loss of clear separation between independent and dependent variables" because:

> Each subject's behavior is at the same time a response to a past behavior of the other and a stimulus to a future behavior of the other; each behavior is in part dependent variable and in part independent variable; in no clear sense is it properly either of them [307].

In summary, the transactional approach to dyadic communication stresses that:

1. Communication is contextual.
2. Each participant simultaneously creates and deciphers communication cues.
3. Each participant affects and is affected by the other.
4. In a communicative transaction, any variable can be seen as independent or dependent, contingent on your point of view.

From the transactional perspective, the simplicity of a dyadic relationship disappears, and communicative transactions are seen as

---

*One may wish to argue, however, that some static variables such as the participants' sex cannot be considered as dependent variables. But such possible variables are very few in number.

in-process, circular, and unrepeatable. The function of this book is to illustrate the transactional, relationship-bound nature of the dyadic communication process.*

CHARACTERISTICS OF DYADS

Imagine yourself sitting alone in the library or at home and a friend approaches. Whether you were reading, daydreaming, or simply gazing at the sky, a reorientation is necessary with the arrival of your friend. You have to take account of the other person's presence; there is a change "away from the comfort and safety of self-preoccupation and toward a more inclusive frame of reference that embraces the experiential field of another person" [205]. The presence of the other person constitues another, entirely different social situation. The ensuing discussion, therefore, is qualitatively different from your intrapersonal communication. Both you and your friend have altered behaviors due to reckoning with each other's presence. As Von Wiese [320] noted, ". . . the pair always behaves otherwise than either member would if alone . . . ." A distinctive communication system has been set into motion, a dyadic system.† This distinctiveness is best understood by comparing dyadic communication to other communication contexts.

Of all forms of communicative exchange, dyadic communication is the most prevalent. Observations of people in playgrounds, train depots, shopping malls, and other settings have confirmed that most groupings of people are dyadic [137]. Paul Fischer [89], after a study of college student communication, concluded that the "great bulk of human interaction is dyadic in nature." If you keep a diary of the number of communicative contacts you have with others, you should not be surprised to discover that you have more dyadic contacts, and of longer duration, than any other single type of exchange. While participation in small groups, public speech gatherings, and mass-media arenas are certainly numerous, they are usually outnumbered

---

*For more detailed treatments of the transactional point of view see [18, 19, 73, 76, 133, 205, 222, 279, 281, 315, 334, 341]

†The specific attributes of dyadic transactions from the systems point of view are considered in Chapter 4, "The Nature of Dyadic Relationships."

by the dyadic transactions. In fact, as will be noted later, dyadic pairings are so pervasive that small groups and larger gatherings contain multiple dyadic relationships.

Not only are dyadic relationships most prevalent, our earliest human relationships are dyadic. In early childhood, from two to five years, a person has the ability to engage in communication with only one person at a time. It is not until later childhood, from six to twelve years, that one can engage in communication with several persons at a time [246]. Chronologically speaking, dyadic communication is the primary form of social exchange. As noted above, even after we reach maturity dyadic relationships are so primary that very few individuals live apart from dyadic relationships. In fact, husband-wife, friend-friend, and other social pairs are so prominent that one sociologist concludes, ". . . the human pair is the structure upon which a great many social processes are based, and may be regarded, metaphorically speaking, as the cell-unit in the social structure" [320].

Intimacy.   Of all possible combinations of people, dyadic relationships are the most intimate. It is within the one-to-one situation that the most personal aspects of each participant are presented. The informality of the dyadic context allows the uniqueness of each person more expression than does any other communication context. As a result, intimate behavior that is appropriate within a dyadic context is often disapproved of in public settings. Watch the reactions of people who encounter a romantic pair embracing and kissing while on a heavily traveled public sidewalk. Some onlookers giggle and others are offended, but both reactions arise from dyadic intimacies being displayed in public.

The intimacy of dyadic pairings is not limited to public displays of affection. Intimacy also means that each dyadic relationship we enter into is unique, a product of two distinctive participants. As a result, the intimacy is reflected by each dyad developing its own norms or rules for behavior. I distinctly remember when I was in the eighth grade—Jack and I, both loudmouths, sat next to each other in all our classes. In one class we would giggle no matter what the teacher did. The more inappropriate it was to laugh, the more uncontrollable the urge to giggle was. Finally the teacher, being of rather keen insight, got the best of us. He told me that if Jack spoke out of turn in class or giggled, I could hit Jack on the arm. Jack was given the same instruction. There we sat for the rest of the year—perfect gentlemen with striking arms poised. Because each dyad, like Jack and I, develops its own rules of behavior, these norms for behavior may often run counter to societal norms. In fact, many people form friendships because the standards they adopt as a pair are unconventional or improper [297]. The intimate nature of dyadic transactions makes it possible to develop and maintain a way of life that most others would frown at.

Anyone who has changed close friends can attest to the uniqueness of each dyadic relationship brought on by intimacy. Think of the relationships you are now engaged in. Is your friendship with John similar to the one with Duane? Do you react the same way to Jason that you do to Carina? Are your relationships with men the same as those with women? Of course not! Your dyadic relationships are unique because they are intimate. In each relationship, you and the other invest part of yourselves. And your behavior changes in each case. Can you imagine, for example, using the same tone of voice and words to express the same idea to a friend, your parents, and your favored loved one? What is appropriate in one case is inappropriate in another. What is a good response from you in one situation would be considered a rebuff in the next. And as everyone who is in love knows, there has never been a relationship quite like theirs [183].

Dyadic intimacy has its consequences. The intimacy brings with it the potential for ecstasy or agony. In all types of pairs—love, friendship, family, or common interest—treating the other with respect and warmth is a common occurrence. A close friend, with a touch on our shoulder, can "break down isolation" and change our "condition of solitariness for one of personal intimacy" [320]. In the dyadic transaction, each person can assimilate as much as possible of the other's personality and meet their needs. It is no coincidence that relationships formed for the express purpose of helping someone are dyadic in nature. Institutionalized programs such as Big Brother and Crisis Center set up pairs for the purpose of helping. Other dyadic helping situations are priest-confessor, counselor-client, father-son, mother-daughter, and teacher-student, to name only a few. In all these cases, the pairing can provide for personableness and warmth.

A pair can also plunge to the depths of conflict and unfulfillment. A casual visit to married friends who "are on the outs" can make a miserable evening for anyone. When a dyadic relationship is disintegrating and the participants are in open conflict, the intimacy of the dyad becomes ugly. Spoken endearments give way to blows below the belt. Because the participants know each other well, they know where to strike in anger. The classic confrontations in our society—son and father, husband and wife, employer and employee, lover and lover, child and child—are dyadic. The close bond of the pair can work against them, and the intimacy and personableness of their transactions makes for serious conflict. Dyadic transactions, then, because of their intimacy, have the potential to be the most and least pleasant of situations. You may not always "hurt the one you love," but you have more ability to harm that person than someone with whom you are not on personal terms. To have a significant effect on the other, whether it be pain or pleasure, comes about through the intricate web that dyadic communication spins.

The intimacy of dyads creates a strange paradox—disagreement that arises from the intimacy is typically tempered. Most people realize the potential for destructive impact and, as a result, try to camouflage disagreement. Studies on laboratory dyads conducted by Bales and Borgatta [16] demonstrate "low rates of showing disagreement and antagonism and . . . high rates of asking for information and opinion." In short, there is a hesitancy to respond in evaluative terms. Persons placed in pairs for purposes of the experiment apparently were aware of the potential they had for inflicting injury on the other member of the pair. In a dyadic relationship, whether in the laboratory or outside, each person "recognizes an obligation to protect the ego, the interests and the reputation of the other" [51].

While disagreement is often kept below the surface, a participant is not free to ignore the other. The same bond between participants that puts the damper on emerging tension creates a need for positive feedback. There is a human *need* for feedback [334]. We want others to respond to us, usually favorably. Because of the need for response from others, the lack of a positive response can be just as disrupting to a dyad as a negative one. If your fellow participant exercises undue restraint or aloofness, or sounds as though he is giving a public speech to you, the encounter will undoubtedly be less than satisfying. It is easy to understand why the Bales and Borgatta research found what it did. Dyadic relationships are the most intimate ones available to us. We all have a need for positive responses from others, and we recognize that others do too. Therefore, when we disagree with someone, an easy route to take is to suppress the full extent of the disagreement and to ask for information and opinion. All the responses to another we have discussed, whether demonstrating care and concern, engaging in open interpersonal warfare, or suppressing disagreement, all emanate from the inherent intimacy of the dyad.

Completeness.   All dyadic groupings bring with them a sense of completeness. This characteristic of dyads is reflected in two ways: (1) A dyad often functions as a completed unit, and (2) a dyad cannot be subdivided. Once you and another person have formed a pair, a unique and complete social system results. People both inside and outside particular pairs recognize that the pair can be addressed as a complete unit. Marital pairs, for example, often present a united front to the world—if you want to deal with one member, you have to deal with them both. Such alliances, even if they are temporarily frustrating to outsiders, are very functional. One of the advantages of dyadic relationships is that the strength of both members is pooled; they form an intact unit.

We are so accustomed to reacting to a pair as a pair that totally individualistic behavior of pair members causes us to wonder. Take, for example, a married "couple" that rarely acts as a pair. Each person goes his and her own way and rarely, if ever, is a united front presented. Many people, in reacting to such married arrangements, typically ask, "Why are they married? They certainly do not act in any way committed to each other." Obviously the marriage meets certain needs or it would not continue. But in any event, we expect dyads to at times act as units because dyads typically do.

When a pair acts as an intact social unit, the members can collectively resist outside social pressure. The chosen living styles of a man and a woman can, if the pair chooses, go against accepted standards. If they as a pair support each other and treat the unit as inviolate, then it will probably be so. On the other hand, if a partner does not actively work to support the pair, severe strains will develop. Take the case of two close friends. If one member of the pair seizes every opportunity to criticize the other, to talk "behind his back," such behavior is seen as destructive. If a pair is to remain strong, the members must support each other. Sometimes the mutual support may be a false front. A pair may appear close-knit to others outside it, even though they are not really close. Such cases of "shoulder to shoulder when attacked" and yet "civil war when the outer danger passes by" [320] demonstrate the utility that dyadic bonds have. Dyads are intact units; they can resist social pressure and be a separate social system apart from all others.

Dyads also have a completeness about them because they cannot be subdivided. Each person is confronted only by the other. If you are a member of a pair and are frustrated by the other's behavior, you have limited options. You can deal with it yourself, forsake the relationship and destroy the dyad, or introduce new members. Basically, however, you really have only two choices. You can deal with it yourself or change the dyad. If you introduce a third party, you have dramatically altered the fundamental pair—you have made it a triad and changed the entire system. An important feature of a dyad, therefore, is that if it is to remain intact you *cannot appeal to majority opinion*. There are only two of you and you cannot appeal to others to put pressure on your partner, as is possible in a small group. Importantly, each person "possesses power to influence the decision by withdrawal or veto" [16]. There are only two of you and with the withdrawal of one from the relationship, the pair will cease to exist. In all other forms of social intercourse, the loss of a member will not necessarily mean its destruction, although it will undoubtedly change the system. Even an important position such as President of the United States is easily filled once it is vacated. Larger organizations have a collective identity that keeps them going after an individual is lost. Granted, the character and style of the organization will change with the new replacements, but its life will continue. In a sense, it is immortal. Not so with the dyad. It has no "super-individual structure" to maintain it after one participant leaves [51, 320, 343].

In a dyad, the loss of one is the loss of all. The marked degree of interdependence each member of a dyad has on the other is often only fully realized with a sudden loss. The unexpected death of a loved one can be a shattering experience. The other person is irreplaceable; no other partner can be to you what this one was. As Von Wiese [320] notes, "Occasionally, the survivor and his intimates realize for the first time how far-reaching the effect of the deceased partner upon their previous behavior had been." Unlike a corporation or other large group that finds a replacement for the lost person, the dyad is dead. The surviving member has to initiate a totally new system, complete with new behaviors and adjustments. In sum, each individual is vital to the dyad; it cannot be subdivided.

Distinctiveness From Larger Groups.   The dyad is the building block of other communication contexts. Within small groups of people, each individual engages in a global relationship to others and specific dyadic relationships [305]. It seems that our shifting dyadic relationships allow us to select manageable sets of relationships within a complex social structure. In large, complex organizations such as the military, there is a recognition of the importance of dyadic components. The "buddy" system flourishes within the confines of a larger grouping. But as fundamental as the dyad is, it also has some characteristics that make it distinct from groups that have more than two members. These features can best be highlighted by specifically comparing dyads to small groups.

A collection of three or more individuals constitutes a small group [334]. And while the dyad is obviously the "scheme, germ and material" of small groups [343], it is *qualitatively different* from them. We have already noted the intimacy characteristic of dyads. Compared to small groups, therefore, dyads provide each participant with more involvement, more satisfaction, and more participation [217].

In addition, when a group numbers three or more, the basic properties of all larger groups begin to emerge. Leadership functions become more identifiable, communication networks are established, and coalitions or subsystems are formed [217]. And importantly, majority opinion can be appealed to as a tactic to change another participant's point of view. The addition of new members to a face-to-face transaction dramatically changes the nature of the system.

Let's examine a bit more closely some of the consequences of adding more people to a social setting. To begin with, as the number of people increases arithmetically, the number of possible relationships increases geometrically. With three people A, B, and C, there are six possible relationships between individuals and between individuals and subgroups (A-B, A-C, B-C, AB-C, AC-B, and BC-A). Hare [116] has conveniently figured out the potential relationships in groups from two to seven (see Fig. 1-2).

Size of group	Potential relationship
2	1
3	6
4	25
5	90
6	301
7	966

Fig. 1-2 Potential relationships within groups. *

It is no wonder, then, that as the number of people increase, the situation becomes considerably more complicated than any relationship between two individuals [161]. Each individual has more relationships to maintain in a given amount of time. And it is not surprising when you look closely at Fig. 1-2 that many neurotics and psychotics are able to maintain one-to-one situations but "are unable to consider multiple relationships simultaneously" [249]. Such an array of possibilities is difficult enough for a "well-adjusted" person to comprehend.

The increase in the number of potential relationships is handled in the following typical manners by most groups. Since it is unlikely that all the members can "share the same mood or enter into synchronized sets" [307], two things usually happen. First, as noted above, leadership emerges because it can reduce the psychologically complicated relationships. Group transactions can be reduced to a series of pair relationships of each member with the leader [116], thereby simplifying the communication process. Second, a group typically gains stability by breaking into smaller groups, usually of even-numbered sizes [89].

As the group size increases, the degree of intimacy decreases. The dependency of the group on each individual decreases; a member

---

*Kephart [147] provided a formula to determine the number of potential relationships as a consequence of group size:

$$PR = \frac{3^N - 2^{N+1} + 1}{2},$$

where PR is the number of potential relationships, and N is the number of persons in the group.

or two is easily replaced. And the consequences of alienating a single member become less severe [281]. While each member must fit into a more elaborate structure, he gains psychological freedom and may even "withdraw from the fray without loss of face" [281]. The larger the group, the more disagreement that is shown [351]. Clearly, when compared to larger groups of people, dyads are distinct. Dyadic behavior is unique and different from behaviors in larger groups [351].

THE TRIAD: DYADIC IN NATURE

The distinctive characteristics of dyadic transactions have been sketched above by comparing two-person exchanges to those in small groups. The smallest of small groups, the triad, will now come under intense scrutiny as a backdrop for our continued analysis of the nature of dyadic transactions. It will soon be apparent that one of the most prominent features of triads is the presence of dyadic transactions.

Is a Triad Possible?   A triad is a social system composed of three people transacting face-to-face. On the surface it would appear that a triad functions as a complete entity—each person transacting with each other one. Such an analysis of communication in a triad can best be represented graphically. Figure 1–3 represents a truly triadic relationship. Each outward curve represents a person, and as you can see, they are all joined together.

The three people are obviously intertwined with one other. Such a pure set of relationships, however, rarely if ever exists. A triad, as represented in Fig. 1–3, where "the power and influence of all three members are equal, *is not normal, but on the contrary is extraordinarily rare*" [320]. In a triad, it is normal for one member to be isolated, suppressed, or excluded from complete participation. There exists a primary dyad plus the third person. As an example, a close friendship is forged within a dyadic framework. Friends must close off others in some respects, otherwise their relationship cannot foster and become special in its own right. "If friends invite all others into their private morality, then they lose the very special convenant they have authored" [297]. Look at your own relationships for a moment. Do you have two friends who are also themselves good friends? Do the three of you enjoy doing things as a threesome? If two of you are together, does the sudden appearance of the third make the friendship really blossom, or does it cause an uneasy feeling in you? Probably the latter case is true.

Fig. 1–3   A triadic relationship.*

From a functional standpoint (looking at the relationships), *there is no such thing as a triad*; there is only a primary dyad plus one. There is no triadic relationship that is so stable and complete that "each individual may not, under certain circumstances, be regarded by the other two as an intruder . . ." [278]. Further, it is extraordinarily rare and difficult for three people to come into a "really united state of feeling, which, however, may occur with relative ease between two" [278]. Even our English language makes it difficult to deal with a triadic relationship. We speak and write in first, second, and third person, I am; you are; he is. But this is not the case in face-to-face communication.

---

*Fig. 1–3 is from *The Work of M. C. Escher*, Meredith Press, 1967, p. 36.

I speak to you, and you speak to me, but even by our language, he is separated from us. You and I, if combined, become we. The only way a third person can become one of us is to cease to be a third person; that is, he must join us (first person plural), or he must become one of you (second person plural). By this process, any three people in a persistent situation must form, not a triad, but a dyad of me and you (plural) or you (singular) and us [62].

The most comprehensive and exciting treatment of the nature of triads is by Caplow [51]. His position is that "the most significant property of the triad is its tendency to divide a coalition of two members against the third."* When a primary dyad forms within the framework of three people, it is not necessarily permanent, however. A father, mother, and child, for example, probably will experience shifting alliances. Father and mother may unite against the child to discipline him or her, and the next moment mother and child may argue together for a trip to the forest. Or father and child may join forces in order to go fishing together. The important point is this: When three people are in a face-to-face transaction, the transaction *at any point in time* is composed of a primary dyad plus one.

A Triad Dissected.   Let's take a look at what relationships can be formed within a triad. The three individuals will be labeled A, B, and C. Caplow [51] states that every triad has three relationships: A–B, B–C, and A–C (see Fig. 1–4).

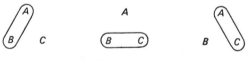

Figure 1–4

You will recall that earlier, however, the small group of three people was said to have *six* relationships [116]. Caplow was only looking at the basic dyadic bonds. In a triad, there are combinations of relationships such that a dyadic pair can relate to the third person. Figure 1–5 shows the range of possible relationships in a triad.

---

*The title of his book alone is instructive: *Two Against One: Coalitions in Triads.*

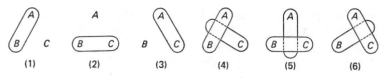

Figure 1–5

In a triad there are six possible relationships, but the seventh possible relationship, shown earlier in Fig. 1–3, is so extraordinarily rare that any of us would be hard pressed to supply an example of one. A related point needs to be made. Diagrams 4, 5, and 6 in Fig. 1–5 show that a triad functionally may consist of *two dyads*. In diagram 4, for example, person C is trying to communicate with A and B. If A and B have formed into a strong coalition, then C has to treat them as a *single unit*. A–B as a unit makes joint decisions and C has to relate to them as if they were a single person who has gained extra strength. The A–B bond is one dyad and the AB–C relationship is the second.

The triad has a tendency to resolve itself into the basic form of a dyad plus one. Because the triad does not exist as portrayed in Fig. 1–3 and tends to dissolve itself into a dyad plus one, *the triad is less stable than a dyad* [306]. There is an innate tendency toward discord.

Enter the Third Party.   The presence of a third person always has an affect on an existing dyad. Whether the dyad is permanent or transitory, the presence of a third person brings *change* [320]. That third person alters the existing "habits in perception, evaluation, and transmission" [246]. We have all experienced the intrusion of a third party into dyads that are transitory. Have you ever been with a close friend having coffee and engrossed in a conversation when a third person approaches? You are stuck. You can tell the third person, "Beat it, I don't want you destroying our dyad!" or do as most of us and say, "Oh, no, you aren't disturbing us. Pull up a chair." There you are, in the middle of a conversation, and you are suddenly faced with a choice. You can ignore the third person, thereby making him feel uncomfortable, or you can stop the conversation and try to bring the third party up-to-date and include him in the conversation. Either choice poses difficulties. One way of coping with the situation would be to do what a friend of mine did. Bob was talking with Cinda when Jeanne joined them. He stopped his conversation right in the middle of a sentence and changed topics as a way to adjust to Jeanne's presence When she left in a few minutes, he turned to Cinda and completed his unfinished sentence, their conversation only temporarily interrupted. It is an ingenious way to deal with an intrusion, but few of us develop such an ability.

When third parties enter existing dyads, whether they are transitory or permanent dyads, they "exert pressures that tend to develop, arrest, maintain, and dissolve . . . the relationships" [153]. One of two things happen: Either the existing dyad is *strengthened* or it is *destroyed*.

One For Two: Strengthening the Dyad.   The presence of a third party can often be the impetus needed for cementing a dyadic bond. When marital couples seek the assistance of a marriage counselor, they are trying to find a third party who can intervene and strengthen their marriage. Oftentimes, too, couples will have a child in the hopes that the baby will provide a bridge over the troubled marital waters. The hope is that the relationship will be intensified by the presence of a third element. The dyad need not be permanent for the third party to provide needed support. Buford and Wallace were having a rather intense argument one evening about how one can do best in his chosen profession. The third person present was Roz, a close friend of Buford's. The dyad consisted of Wallace and Buford, and Roz was in a position to occasionally interrupt and say, "That's right! That's exactly what I said once." She served the function of keeping the Buford-Wallace dyadic communications flowing smoothly. The role of counselor, third-party friend, or mediator are all essentially the same—the presence of this third element can sometimes help strengthen a dyad.

Ironically, if a third person is out to destroy an existing dyad, he may instead strengthen it. The person may provide a "common object of opposition" for the dyad [199]. Whether it is the landlord trying to promote marital disharmony or a third "mutual friend" always getting in the way of two good friends, the original dyadic bonds may be strengthened by the intrusion of the third person. Many human relationships are formed and strengthened because of a mutual dislike for a third party. Many a student has found a new friend because of a mutual dislike for the professor in a required class. The effect of such rejection of a third person is to make the dyadic bond stronger, becoming the justification for it. If *A* and *B* reject *C* and feel closer because of it, then they can easily conclude that because they feel close to each other, they should not let C into their inner circle.

Two Against One: Fighting It Out.   The other major effect of the presence of a third person is the destruction, or attempted destruction, of the existing dyad. The third party often tries to "divide and conquer." He wants to disrupt the dyad so he can have a partner. Simmel [343] calls it "Tertius Gaudens", because the third party is striving for his own ends. This type of situation has two main variants:

> Either two parties are hostile toward one another and therefore compete for the favor of a third element; or they compete for the favor of a third element and therefore are hostile toward one another [343].

Whatever the chain of events, if the original dyad is disrupted, the third person finds a partner and a new pair is formed.

Most of us have participated in triadic situations when the presence of the third person causes disruption. For example, were you ever in a situation with a boyfriend or girlfriend and a younger brother joins you? Or have you ever tried to have a meaningful talk with a boyfriend or girlfriend with your mother in the room? Such feelings of discomfort are not limited to romantic pairs. Mac and Bob were close friends but Bob had another very close friend, Wes. Once when Mac was upset over something about Bob, he remarked, "I don't like the way Bob acts when he is with Wes." In other words, Mac did not care for the Bob-Wes dyad because it meant that Mac was the third person, the outsider.

Any dyad is potentially disruptable by a third person. If two college seniors are engaged to be married and the man begins to establish close professional ties with a favored professor, the young lady can be expected to have some negative reaction. Think of the times you have been excluded, ignored, or brushed aside because a person close to you preferred to spend time with a third person. The feeling of exclusion can cause severe hurt at times.

To pretend that the introduction of a third party will not affect an existing dyadic relationship is sometimes to court disaster. A husband and wife who are very close, enjoy hiking together, and doing other things on the spur of the moment are kidding themselves if they think having a child will not affect their relationship. The child may cause the father to compete for the mother's affection (or vice versa), thereby introducing an entirely new dimension into the relationship. When the child gets older it is distinctly possible that one parent will form a more-or-less permanent bond with the child, excluding the previous partner. To pretend that the arrival of a baby will not affect the couple's relationship is to ignore the reality of all triads. At a given point in time, *someone* is the excluded third party.

The most dramatic example of the effects of a third party occurs when the wife's mother comes to visit or live with the wife and husband. The situation confronts the wife with a dilemma. She essentially has to choose between "two valuable coalitions, one indispensable in her family of origin and the other in the family she has entered" [51]. If she forms a coalition with her mother, the husband will feel alienated; if she forms a coalition with her husband, her mother will feel alienated. Someone will be regarded by the other two as an intruder, because as was demonstrated earlier, the triad naturally breaks into a dyad plus one. *Three people cannot fully enter into the same mood.* The difficulty with the mother-in-law coming to visit or to live results from the fundamental characteristic of triads being composed of a dyad plus one. This effect is not limited to our culture. In other cultures, perhaps because they understand triadic relationships, specific prohibitions are placed on socialization between men and their mothers-in-law:

> In more than three-fifths of the world's societies, severe penalties follow upon the meeting of a man and his mother-in-law, and they shun each other accordingly. In northern Australia, a man who speaks to his mother-in-law must be put to death. In parts of the South Pacific, both parties would commit suicide. In Yucatan, men believe that to meet one's mother-in-law face to face would render a man sterile for life, so he may travel miles out of his way over dangerous territory to avoid being near her. Navaho men believe that they will go blind if they see their mothers-in-law, so that she is not even allowed to attend the wedding" [51].

It may not be wise for our culture to impose such penalties, but we should certainly be aware of the high possibility for discord when a third element is introduced. We may wish to pay the price, or we may wish to see a dyad disrupted. But in any event, we should be aware of the tension caused by triadic transactions.

One more anecdote. Arnie and Orlie both wanted to win the favor of Diane. All three of them met at the same time, but as a result of earlier conversations, Orlie and Diane began to like each other. Arnie, the perfect example of a "Tertius Gaudens" because he had his own welfare at stake, wanted to pair up with Diane. The scene was set for the perfect triangle. Arnie, however, being a discerning and warm human being, did not want to wage open warfare. For three days in a row, he invited Orlie and Diane out for lunch. There they went to lunch like one big happy family. Arnie's dealings with the existing dyad did not diminish the ever-strengthening bond between Orlie and Diane. After Arnie left town, the original pair was still a pair. The attempt to alter the dyadic alliance was unsuccessful.

Which Dyad Will Form?   The dyad that forms within a triad does so for specific reasons. When you pair up with another, it is a clear case of choice because, theoretically, each person has two partners from which to pick. A dyadic coalition arises in a triad so that paired members can affect the outcomes. Two children gang up against a third precisely because they can, by joining together, increase their influence over the third. A husband and wife pair up so as to better discipline their child (and the child tries to pair up with one parent to avoid discipline). A close dyadic friendship, regardless of whether it forms within a triad or not, serves the same function as a coalition in a triad. We know that a friend will come to our aid, and we will to his. In effect, we form a coalition so that power resources of the friendly pair can be mobilized against an external threat [307]. A dyad can be viewed as a coalition formed for the purpose of maximizing desired outcomes.

Within a triad, what types of coalitions will form? One study demonstrated that the two more active members form the pair, and the isolated individual is the one who is least active [199]. Within families where sibling rivalry is present, the typical coalitions involve siblings of the same sex and children closest in age [51]. Overall, peers often select each other on the basis of likeness; those who are the most alike form pairs [51]. In purely economic terms, a person wishing to maximize his financial gain is often confronted with a choice. He can choose a less effective coalition in which he is powerful, or a powerful coalition in which he is less effective [307]. One person expressed his choice this way: "I'd rather have ten percent of a million dollars than one-hundred percent of ten dollars."

Predicting coalition formation is still far from an exact science. The most comprehensive treatments of available research do not set forth definitive conclusions. However, some experimental work on dyadic formation is interesting. A, B, and C are three people who play a laboratory game, the goal of which is to maximize rewards. The Vinacke-Arkoff game (see Fig. 1–6) is a sample of experimental predictions. Note that the size of the circles corresponds to the weights assigned to each player by the experimenter.

Such experiments demonstrate that in laboratory simulations, persons with excessively high or excessively low power (assigned weights) do not form coalitions. In the real world, however, the "payoffs" we will receive rarely are clearly specified. Furthermore, a host of other factors undoubtedly affect coalition formation besides striving for rewards. One point seems clear, however. A triad functions with a coalition, but it cannot function with two coalitions at the same time [51]. The husband-wife-wife's mother coalition is a case in point—when all three people are transacting, the wife cannot be a partner with both husband and mother at the same time.

Dyadic coalitions in triads are *not necessarily permanent*. They can, and often do, shift back and forth. If a dyad is permanently formed against a third party in a family, the prolonged rejection of the third party can be devastating. As Hare [116] says, ". . . members tend to switch coalitions from one disagreement to another simply to maintain solidarity and avoid the permanent exclusion of one member." Similarly, most of us can cite instances of dyads we enter into and exit from periodically.

Dyads always form within triads. In fact, because the dyad is the basic unit of social exchange, it is the fundamental building block upon which triadic relationships form.

SUMMARY

Dyadic communication is a transactional process. Each participant's perception of the other is a transaction between the qualities of the other and his unique interpretation of them. Furthermore, when the two participants are in the presence of each other, they are both creating and deciphering communication cues. As a result, each participant affects and is affected by the other.

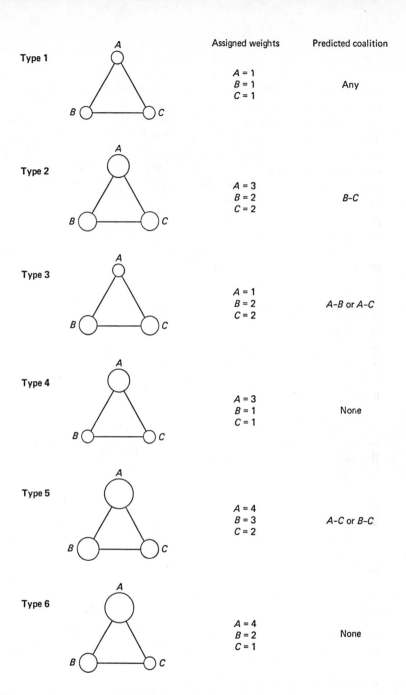

Fig. 1-6 Predicted coalition formation.

While dyadic encounters are distinct from larger groupings of people (they are more intimate and far less complex), they do form the building blocks of larger groupings. The triad consists of a primary dyadic coalition plus another person who has not fully entered into the coalition's mood. Even larger groupings are also characterized by shifting dyadic relationships. The study of dyadic communication exposes the communication process to examination in its most basic and prevalent context.

Chapter 2
Perception of the Self

"Grandfather," asked the grandson, "why is it that people often aren't what they seem?"

"Do people seem to be what they aren't to you?" the old man replied.

"Yes, sometimes they do," the grandson said.

The grandfather pondered, as though he had once asked a question much like the one he was now to answer. "Young man, it must be remembered that in being human, we have no choice but to rely only upon our perceptions of what appears to be real. Thus appearances, not realities, form the foundation for all our observations of behavior. And, in determining which people seem more real than others, and why they appear as they do, it is the perception of one's self that is important above all things. For to be skilled in observing others, one must first be skilled in observing himself."

Again the grandfather pondered. His eyes shone and he caught the other's eyes with their brightness. "Young man?" he asked with a grin, "Do I seem real to you?"

The grandson hesitated, reflecting on the discussion which had begun only moments before. "You appear to be," he replied. "Am I correct?"

"Very perceptive," the older responded with yet a bigger grin than before.

"But what of myself, grandfather?" the younger continued with a voice of concern. "Do I also appear to be real? And if so, how do I know this?"

"You appear to be real to me," the grandfather said. "Do you know why? Because you seem to believe in yourself and your thoughts, and are willing to let this be known to others. It is their preceptions of how you view yourself that will aid you in telling whether you are perceived as being real or not. And the kinds of relationships you will experience with others are a result of these perceptions. It is wise, my grandson, to never forget that one's relations with others are forever dependent upon one's perceptions of himself."

The younger remained silent, and the older said, "You seem puzzled by my answers to your questions. Am I not correct?"

"Very perceptive!" the grandson replied laughingly, hoping to catch the elder's response with his glance. "But I must go now,

33

and have no time to discuss what I do not understand. Will you remember what you have spoken until I come again?"

"I will try," the grandfather quietly responded, already looking forward to the young man's next visits.*

The story of the grandfather and grandson is an apt beginning for our discussion of self-perception. It makes us aware that we act toward ourselves and others based in part on our perceptions of ourselves. Furthermore, the meanings that we have for ourselves are derived from our transactions with others. The basic components upon which all dyadic transactions are structured, perception of the self and perception of the other, are the topics of this and the following chapters.

It is fascinating that we have the ability to attach meaning to our own behavior.† The ability to analyze oneself may, in fact, be man's most distinctive characteristic. While other members of the animal kingdom can respond, it is not at all certain that they can be self-reflexive. The ability to engage in self-reflexive acts is best stated by Allport [4]:

We are not only aware of what is peculiarly ours, but we are also aware that we are aware.

Whether man is the only creature capable of self-reflexive thinking or not, this ability has a profound effect on his dyadic relationships. As this chapter will demonstrate, our self-concepts are inextricably bound to our relationships with others, both influencing them and influenced by them.

The self-concept is a generalized view of oneself that is obviously subjective. Whatever an individual thinks he is, *to him* this *is* what he is [310]. Take the case of Mike, a student in an interpersonal communication class. He is in his words, "an upper middle-class

---

*Reprinted by permission of Wayne Beach.

†George H. Mead [193] distinguishes between man as subject (being aware of things) and as object (being the thing you are aware of). While his distinction was useful for emphasizing that man can have a conception of himself, it introduces so many philosophical and semantic tangles that it has not been developed here.

Black with connections." He is very bright, outgoing, and genuinely friendly to others in the class. It came as a shock to us to discover one day that Mike saw himself as shy and afraid to talk to people. He was quite serious; he really saw himself as shy and retiring. His meaning for himself was not at all what any one of us would have guessed.

The subjective nature of the self-concept is manifested in other ways as well. For instance, two individuals can have similar experiences yet will have totally different meanings for them. One student can flunk a test and it will signal for him that "it's time to get busy," while a second person will interpret the same grade as meaning "you are no good." One self-concept has been bolstered and the other has been badly shaken because the meanings are subjective and internal to that particular person.

COMPONENTS OF THE SELF-CONCEPT

Each person's self-concept is subjective primarily because (1) there are differing degrees of awareness of the self, and (2) we each have "multiple selves" from which to choose.

Degrees of Self-Awareness.   Most people accept their lives and the meanings of their lives as given, reflecting on these meanings only when a novel situation develops. Novel situations that promote re-flexive thinking are quite disparate. If, for example, you have just experienced a disruption in a relationship, self-reflexive thinking occurs. A newly divorced man or woman, or someone who finds himself the outsider in a romantic triad, is typically the one who be-gins to question his self-concept. Questions like "If I'm normal, then why didn't it work?" are quite serious at such times. Even the disrup-tion of a potential dyadic relationship can lead to self-examination. The person who asks a romantic partner to live with him and is re-fused will probably engage in some self-examination. Or take the case of the smallest boy in a high school class. If he is the only one who did not make the basketball team, he may subject himself to intensive personal questioning. While the others are on the court giving the game their utmost, he is on the sidelines wallowing in personal re-morse.

Of course, not all novel situations are negative, nor do they all produce a weakened self-concept. For instance, if a wife applies for her first full-time job in years, having spent that time as a full-time homemaker and child raiser, she will probably undergo many self-reflexive moments. If all goes well, she will probably experience an improvement in her self-concept. Abilities she was not quite certain she had prove to exist. Similarly, a move to a new city can bring new friendships and a heightened feeling of personal worth. Whenever novel situations arise, whether they be disasters or good fortunes, an individual will typically become more aware of himself.

One other type of novel situation is worth mentioning because it so frequently occurs. When there is an inconsistency between what you believe and what you have done, awareness of the self is prompted. If you do not believe in stealing but are "talked into it" by some friends, personal examination will be the next step. Or if you do not believe in permarital sexual relations but find yourself engaging in them, self-reflexive thinking will closely follow. Whether you become entangled in personal remorse or spend your time trying to rationalize your behavior, your concept of yourself will undergo some degree of examination.

Not only does our awareness of self change as a result of a novel experience, our own usual degree of awareness may be quite different from someone else's. A self-proclaimed "Mr. Know-it-all" who has no periods of reflection projects quite a different communication behavior from "Mr. Shy," the fellow who rarely speaks. The first fellow may take a close look at himself only once a week, whereas the second fellow scrutinizes himself periodically. And these "peeks at the self" may be quite different. The first undergoes a simple check to see if he put all his clothes on and is still breathing. The second examines himself to the point that he is trapped into reflections about his reflections. He thinks, "Gee, I sure don't impress people with my communicative ability. Anybody who has no ability to communicate has nothing to contribute. And if I have to worry and fret about my communicative ability, I really must be messed up." His reflections about his reflections keep him so internally occupied that his shyness is accelerated.*

---

*This example is only for purposes of illustration. It may not be at all true that vocal and socially aggressive people are less aware of themselves than are more timid folk. Likewise, shyness or lack of social exchange does not necessarily lead to reflections about reflections.

Multiple Selves

"You should have seen Ed at the last convention. He was so blasted he picked a fight. He wasn't himself for two days."

"I don't know about Carrie. She is going to a nude marathon to try and find herself.

"I wish Sam would quit playing games on our dates. He is always trying to impress me with his intelligence. If he would just be himself, we'd get along a lot better."

What are you *really* like? Your teacher thinks you are too easy-going, your friends feel you take life too seriously, and your parents quite probably think you are too rebellious. How do you go about finding the *real* you? Is it the *real* you showing when you are drunk, stoned, or in love? Or is it the *real* you sitting under a tree all by yourself thinking about life?

There is no real you, and a search for it is doomed to fail. A complex human being, subjected to different people and pressures, is no solitary blob of identity. Each of us is complex; the person one is on the job or at school is different from the one in the company of a close friend. The impressions others have of us are, at best, incomplete and slightly faulty, and so are the impressions we have of ourselves.

Obviously all of us are complex, and there are innumerable components or parts of our lives that affect our self-concepts. As an example, let's take a superficial look at John. For his self-concept, he can pick from any or all of the following characteristics (plus many more):

- Tall
- From Cozad, Nebraska
- Well-liked
- Doesn't have to shave much
- Has a Ph.D.
- Husband
- Father of three
- Drives a Ford
- Hard-working
- Friendly
- Close friend of Bill
- Author
- Sensitive
- Needs others
- Others need him
- Successful

The list could include thousands more items. And John can choose from all his attributes, possessions, and experiences (and future goals) to make up his self-concept.

There are multiple selves. One general semanticist makes the point that self should be represented as: Self-1, Self-2, Self-3, Self-4, . . ., Self-n, ad infinitum [35]. In the case of John, we listed only sixteen aspects of his life. These sixteen qualities could be rank ordered in importance to him, and then combined in all possible ways. For instance, let's say his self-concept was most dependent upon (1) driving a Ford, and (2) having a Ph.D. Another combination could easily be (1) sensitive, (2) has a Ph.D., and (3) drives a Ford. If we put together all possible permutations of just these sixteen items, there would be 20,923,000,000,000 possible configurations he could select from for his self-concept. And that is only from sixteen qualities!

For purposes of understanding, it is useful to look at the components of the self-concept from a broader framework. After all, no one wants to list all possible aspects that can contribute to a generalized view of oneself and then try to figure out all the possible combinations. One of the earliest category systems for describing the self was offered by James [138].* His list was composed of three items:

1. Material self
2. Social self
3. Spiritual self

According to James' point of view, each of us has these three as separate components of our self-concept. The *material self* consists of our body, clothing, and other trappings or material possessions that we see as part of us. The importance of clothes to many people is obvious. Some find it necessary to always "dress to the hilt"; with many present college students, it is important that their clothes *not* be important to them. The importance of the material self in developing the self-concept is easily observed in children. A child extends his sense of self by identifying with his material possessions [5]. Give a young child a set of pistols, boots, and a cowboy hat and shirt, and

---

*Numerous other classifications are available. For example, see [4, 77, 100]. James writes that the material, social, and spiritual selves constitute the empirical self, or "me." The author has taken the liberty of interpreting the empirical self to be the generalized view one has of himself—the self-concept.

he may try to convince you he *is* a cowboy. My own three-year-old son went through a small trauma because his material possessions did not match one aspect of his self-concept. We had just returned from vacationing in Wyoming where he had ridden a horse for the first time. With boots borrowed from a cousin and other appropriate gear, he rode "his" horse. Everything was fine until we returned home and prepared to go to a small-town rodeo. All of a sudden he realized that he no longer had his borrowed boots. He promptly informed me that "*all* cowboys wear boots," making it perfectly clear between tears that without boots he could not be a cowboy. Luckily I was able to convince him that new boots would be forthcoming next year prior to his being a cowboy again in Wyoming.

For some people, the material aspects of their lives are so prominent that the material self is a significant portion of their entire self-concept. The individual who buys objects because of their "image" is simply saying that he wants you as well as himself to conceive of him in a particular way. The overweight man of thirty-three who buys a Porsche may be trying to change his self-concept. He may actually become young and sporty (in his eyes) by the purchase. Many people define themselves by what they own rather than what they do. After all, if you own a 140-dollar high-light tent, a pair of expensive hiking boots, and appropriately faded cut-off jeans, you must be an experienced backpacker and hiker. Most of us, whether we go to the extent described above or not, can find material objects we own that are central to our material self. Whether it be a professor's books, a banker's Cadillac, or a student's stereo set, we all have a material self which is part of our overall self-concept.

The second contributor to each person's self-concept is the *social self*. The social self is the recognition one earns from others, arising out of dyadic and other transactions. The social self is so crucial to everyone's self-concept that the next section in this chapter deals specifically with it. As a short illustration of one aspect of social self, let's examine body identity. The perception you have of how others see your body constitutes your body image. And your body image can be an important contributor to your self-concept. The fact that the human body can "readily be set off as an organic unit" [277] prompts us to be aware of it. However, some people work to suppress the sense of their body. They perceive sexual relations, for example, not as an expression of themselves but merely as an act their body performs. Or in more general terms, they see their body as an object separate from themselves. Rollo May [182] argues convincingly that achieving an awareness of the self begins with experiencing one's body and feelings, often accomplished through the reactions of others. To treat the body as something separate from your "self" is to act as though it were a "truck to be driven until it runs out of gas." May's point is that the more bodily self-awareness one has, the more "alive" he is.

The third and final aspect of the self-concept is the *spiritual self*. For James, the spiritual self included the actions of the psyche, the process of introspection, one's thinking. The spiritual self is made up of all one's intellectual, moral, and religious aspirations. From it arise the sense of moral or mental superiority and, conversely, the sense of inferiority or guilt. While James interpreted the spiritual self in very broad terms, its existence is most easily observed in the narrower sense of religious belief and action. Individuals' self-concepts are affected by how they perceive themselves in the overall scheme of things. For instance, people are often concerned with events that happen before and after death. Your self-concept is affected by how you believe your behavior fits with your spiritual convictions. A person maintains a positive self-concept as long as he maintains a belief system that he perceives as giving him approval [7]. A central belief in God and an adherence to the principles of behavior that one perceives as associated with such a belief can play an important role in one's overall self-concept.

The material, social, and spiritual selves combine in unique ways to constitute each person's estimation of himself. For one person a belief in a personal savior may be the component of his self-concept most crucial to his life. For another person the spiritual self may be relatively unimportant in shaping his overall view of himself. One of the nice things about a complex society is that we can choose between several goals. We each can set our own goals, each one related to different components of the self, and evaluate our success at them. One person can be a poor typist, yet his self-concept does not founder. Another may be overweight, but unless he sets being slim as a worthy goal, his self-concept will not be damaged. We don't all have to be athletes to feel important—neither do we all have to fix a car, take a thirty-mile hike, nor write a book. We can select an appropriate goal for ourselves, perform well at the task, and have a feeling of worth.

As noted, the self-concept is composed of the material, social, and spiritual selves. When one particular goal becomes important to you (fixing a car, having a lot of friends, or attending church), your performance in achieving that goal constitutes your self-esteem. Self-esteem is your feeling of worth arising from a specific situation, and the combination of all cases of specific self-esteem makes up your self-concept. Self-esteem and, in the long run, the self-concept are determined by (1) the goals (pretentions) you set, and (2) your success at accomplishing them. James [138] put it most succinctly:

$$\text{Self-esteem} = \frac{\text{Success}}{\text{Pretentions}}$$

According to this formulation, the person who wants to be a million-aire and makes $40,000 a year will be less happy than a person who wants $20,000 a year and makes $18,000. Interestingly enough, the person who has the most may be less happy due to his lofty goals. And the person who has minimal goals may feel the best about him-self. As an individual who wants to increase your self-esteem, you have two options available: (1) increase your success at the chosen goal (pretention), or (2) lower the goal.

There are two major components of the self-concept. First, the degree of awareness you have of yourself is central to any self-examination. Second, the self has many aspects; they are innumerable. The major types of multiple selves are the material, social, and spiritual. The social self is the one most central to dyadic communication and will now be treated in detail.

THE SOCIAL SELF

Each to each a looking glass
Reflects the other that doth pass [57].

Cooley's famous two-line poem expresses the fact that self-concepts are essentially social in nature. While James (138) noted that the material and spiritual selves contribute to the self-concept, social life is the beginning and sustenance for all the components of the self-concept. The material and spiritual selves have meanings for us be-cause of others around us. Why be concerned with clothes (part of the material self) if others are not around to see them? The meanings one attaches to his thinking about himself (spiritual self) are likewise molded in society. Frankl [93] goes so far as to say that the "true meaning of life" is to be found in the world rather than in one's psyche or spiritual self. In any event, our communication transactions with others mold our self-concept.

Numerous social scientists agree in principle with Cooley's notion of the "looking-glass" self. Following are some short statements which emphasize that our communicative transactions are the cornerstone of the self-concept.

> . . . the sense of identity requires the existence
> of another by whom one is known.
>
> —R. D. Laing

> The self may be said to be made up of reflected appraisals.
>
> —H. S. Sullivan

> It is well to remember that all the information a
> person possesses about himself is derived from
> others. His impression of the impact he had upon
> others is what makes up the picture of himself.
>
> —J. Ruesch

> . . . will conceive of himself much as he believes
> significant others conceive of him.
>
> —C. Gordon and K. Gergen

> The becoming of a person is always a social becoming:
> I become a person as I progress through social situations.
>
> —Tiryakian

> . . . we maintain our natural level of self-esteem
> so long as we do not lose the approval, affection,
> and warmth of those around us.
>
> —L. Woodman

> We are who we are only in relationship to the
> other person(s) we're communicating with.
>
> —J. Stewart

> I am not what I think I am. I am not what you think I am.
> I am what I think you think I am.
>
> —Bleiberg and Leubling

This vitally important social self is built primarily in three ways: (1) by the reflected appraisals of others or the "looking-glass" self, (2) by the comparison of the self with others, and (3) by the playing of social roles.

The Looking-Glass Self.   That the appraisals of others affect us has been demonstrated time and time again. Rosenthal [239], for example, showed that if teachers expected students to be intelligent, the latter performed better in school.* Tell someone he is untalented enough times and he will begin to perceive himself that way. Guthrie [111] and Kinch [149] both relate similar stories which demonstrate the impact that the evaluations of others can have. In the Kinch example, five males in a graduate-level class wanted to see if the notion of the "looking-glass" self could be put to use. The girl in the class who could be described at best as "plain" was their subject. They planned to respond to her as if she were the best-looking girl on campus, and to watch the effects of the treatment. Here is how it went:

> They agreed to work into it naturally so that she would not be aware of what they were up to. They drew lots to see who would be the first to date her. The loser, under the pressure of the others, asked her to go out. Although he found the situation quite unpleasant, he was a good actor and by continually saying to himself "she's beautiful, she's beautiful . . ." he got through the evening. According to the agreement, it was now the second man's turn and so it went. The dates were reinforced by the similar responses in all contacts the men had with the girl. In a matter of a few short weeks the results began to show. At first it was simply a matter of more care in her appearance; her hair was combed more often and her dresses were more neatly pressed, but before long she had been to the beauty parlor to have her hair styled, and was spending her hard-earned money on the latest fashions in women's campus wear. By the time the fourth man was taking his turn dating the young lady, the job that had once been undesirable was now quite a pleasant task. And when the last man in the conspiracy asked her out, he was informed that she was pretty well booked up for some time in the future. It

---

*The concept of the *self-fulfilling prophecy* is treated at length in Chapter 5.

seems that there were more desirable males around than those "plain" graduate students [149].

Besides the poetic justice involved, the impact of others' views are clear. The girl perceived the actual response of the men such that she had to change her self-concept, which in turn changed her behavior. It may be that the entire process works because people need others and need to be needed [334]. Whatever the reason, the way we see others seeing us greatly influences how we see ourselves. It is so important that "no more fiendish punishment could be devised". . . than to be "turned loose on society and remain absolutely unnoticed by all the members thereof" [138].

Self: A Residue.   It should be clear by now that one's self-concept is formed in his social contexts. The examples used to illustrate the development of the self-concept, however, may make it appear that one's self-concept changes in every different social situation. A short description of the *residual self* is therefore in order.

Our self-concept is built by the meanings we attach to all our experiences—those of the past and those we are engaged in now—and the meshing of those meanings with our future aspirations. When we have a communication experience, the interplay between our expectations and how we see people reacting to us adds another element to our self-concept. It must be stressed that the meanings are constructed through selective perception, which is partially governed by our past experiences of social acceptance. It is this *residue* of past experiences, which we retain as meanings, that influences our current reactions.

No one enters a communicative exchange without some form of self-concept. Our views of ourselves are never blank; we always possess a residue of past experiences. If people react to your behavior in consistent ways, then there is no discrepancy between (1) how you saw yourself before the transaction and (2) how you see yourself during and after the transaction. In other words, your self-concept was reinforced in that social relationship [277]. And as Woodman [344] says, we maintain our natural level of self-concept "so long as we do not lose the approval, affection, and warmth of those around us." Even though the self-concept is situationally determined, as long as it is supported it *appears* to be a stable personality trait.

The interplay between the self-concept and a given social situation can be sketched as follows:*

1. You enter a situation with a residual self-concept.
2. Your behavior is experienced by others; their interpretation of your behavior influences theirs.
3. You interpret (attach meaning to) the others' behavior.
4. You view yourself as you think others do based on your meaning for their behavior.
5. When necessary, you reconcile the two views of yourself: (a) the residual self-concept and (b) number (4) above. You arrive at a slightly revised self-concept which is a new residual of the two meanings. And the process continues.

Put simply, the residual self-concept from your previous experiences is balanced against the view of yourself that you have in a particular transaction.

If you see the five-step process above as cyclic, you have perceived it correctly. While it regulates our behavior in a dyadic transaction, the self-concept is also shaped by that transaction. While the concepts of the "looking-glass" self and the residual self give some hints as to this transaction between the self-concept and dyadic experience, a more specific treatment is necessary.

The Cyclic Process. In a dyadic relationship, the self-concepts of both participants are modified and grow out of the communicative exchanges. For purposes of illustration, consider person *A* and person *B* who are close friends. The following perceptions will be operating in their on-going transactions:†

Person *A*	Person *B*
1. I perceive my self.	1. I perceive my self.
2. I perceive *B*'s self.	2. I perceive *A*'s self.
3. I perceive *B* perceiving my self.	3. I perceive *A* perceiving my self.

---

*This is an expansion and revision of the paradigm suggested by Heine[123].

†This is adapted from R.D. Laing's ideas. A more complete presentation of his system for viewing dyadic transactions appears in Chapter 4.

Each person has an idea of what the other thinks of him. Thus each person's self-concept emerges from and is an element of his social transactions.

The cyclic nature of the transaction between the self-concept and dyadic exchanges has been diagramatically presented by Kinch [149]. Take a moment and carefully study Fig. 2–1.

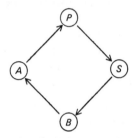

P = perception of other's responses toward him
S = self-concept
B = his behavior
A = actual responses of others toward him

Fig. 2–1 The cyclic nature of the self-concept.

One's self-concept influences his behavior, which of course impacts one the actual responses of the other participant. In turn, your perception of the other's responses develops your self-concept, *ad infinitum*. As Kinch states it, "The individual's concept of himself emerges from social interaction and, in turn, guides or influences the behavior of that individual" [149].

This is the process of interplay as sketched from the viewpoint of one participant. There are two participants engaged in the process, and as a result, a similar description should be provided for the second person. *Each person's view of himself affects his as well as his partner's behavior.* Stated another way, each self-concept influences and is influenced by the communicative transaction.

Very little empirical work has focused on such cyclic processes. For one thing, such a view has yet to gain any general acceptance; its advent is relatively recent. For another, it is difficult in experiments that are designed to ferret out cause-effect relationships to consider the same variable as both independent and dependent. One interesting although not conclusive investigation has paved the way for such approaches. Coombs [59] tested the cyclic model by examining the relationship between social participation, self-concept, and interpersonal valuation (receiving a favorable evaluation from others). Specifically, dancing was the index for social participation, self-concept was measured, and the favorable or unfavorable evaluations of dancing partners were assessed. The partners were paired for the dance on the basis of computerized selection. Coombs discovered that, in general, "previous dating experience increases the probability of being favorably evaluated by a dating partner; favorable evaluations foster a favorable view of self; and a favorable self-concept leads to more participation in dating" [59].

The Coombs investigation was inventive in that it attempted to empirically test the cyclic point of view concerning self-concept and transactions with others. However, it does leave many unanswered questions.* For example, while the cyclic point of view does indicate mutual influences of concept and social transactions, it does not specify that those influences are of equal magnitude. Specifically, since we each enter a dyadic transaction or series of transactions with a residual self-concept, it would be unlikely to find the self-concept undergoing a total change. The degree of influence that the self-concept has on one's transactions, and vice versa, is one of the most challenging issues facing those who wish to understand dyadic communication. In any event, the process of interplay between the self-concept and dyadic transactions is cyclical.

The Self by Social Comparison.   The second subcategory of the social self is the image we build of ourselves by comparison with others. More often than not, the comparison is made with peers.

---

*There were some methodological difficulties which mitigate against full-scale acceptance of the study. For instance, the selected measures of self-concept were not straightforward. Instead of asking the individual what he thought of himself, he was asked what he thought others thought of him. In addition, and more importantly, the same individuals were not selected for each step of the analysis. Rather than following one individual through to see if his participation increased his self-concept which then leads to higher evaluations by others, the analysis took each hypothesis separately. Those individuals who had high evaluations by others had favorable self-concepts. And those who had favorable self-concepts had more participation in dating. But the same individuals were not followed throughout the study.

Sally, the young girl who is concerned about her attractiveness, wants to be invited to an upcoming party. If Sue gets an invitation and Sally doesn't, Sally is painfully aware of how she compares. Similarly, Jack knows he is an excellent student only if he can compare himself to other students for some idea of his relative standing.

A formal theory of social comparison processes has been offered by Festinger [87]. The aspects of the theory that are relevant to our discussion follow. We all have a basic drive to have correct opinions about the world and for accurate self-appraisals. When objective, nonsocial means of evaluation are not available or are ambiguous, we evaluate our opinions and abilities by comparison with others. We often choose peers for comparison because they closely approximate our ability and opinions.

By recalling James' formula for self-esteem, the impact of social comparison on our self-concepts can be made evident. If self-esteem equals success divided by pretentions, determination of degree of success is crucial. How does one arrive at some estimate of his success? By comparison with others. In addition, how does one establish goals or pretentions? By comparison with others. The entire process of establishing self-esteem is dependent upon our comparison with others.* This process takes place in every activity from school, to skiing, to selling life insurance. In fact, when "objective" standards are established for performance (every tenderfoot boyscout has to be able to tie a square knot), these standards arise from the past performance of others.

As a side comment, a person's level of pretentions or goals is affected by his past performance in trying to attain a goal. Furthermore, a person's criteria for his level of success will be modified if he is told of someone else's performance. If he finds that his performance is below that of someone he considers to have little ability, he will raise his goal level. Conversely, if he is performing above someone who he thinks has a great deal of ability, he will lower his aspirations. Whichever is the case, the social comparison with others is another social aspect central to the self-concept.

---

*Obviously, a large part of the comparison to others is based on their reactions, their evaluation of our performance. Even here, the "looking-glass" nature of self-concept plays a part.

Playing Social Roles

> . . . a man has as many social selves as there are
> individuals who recognize him.
>
> —W. James

The complexity of modern society places us in situations that demand
widely different behaviors. When our society was more agrarian, an
individual's niche in the social order was rather firmly established.
The family was the basis of one's identity, and job and home were
closely meshed. Now, however, it is not unusual that our family
members do not even know the people we work with. We are
expected to be effective people in the hustle and bustle of city life and
then, as if by magic, transform ourselves into fully functioning family
members. To our parents we are one person, to our coworkers or
fellow students another, and to our closest loved ones still a third.

An alarm bell has been sounded. Many people perceive our
social lives as tearing us apart, as making us into social chameleons
who change personality with every new situation. Goffman [103], for
example, perceives a person as running around trying to "convey an
impression to others which is in his interests to convey." From his
point of view, we conduct our social relationships as types of calculated performances. We are always playing roles in order to make the
proper impressions. As a result, there is little left in the way of an
identifiable self-concept. The person wears masks and plays his
socialized role "so well that he forgets who he is or what he looks like
when the staged performance is over" [401]. According to this view,
we have an "other-directed" culture where we conform to others'
expectations rather than to any inner sense of values [232]. We become "yes-men" in the organization by adopting the correct lifestyle
and adopt "Yes, J.B., you're right!" behaviors just to please our
superiors [338]. In the current lingo, we sell ourselves out to the social
order.

However, we do have to adjust to the presence of others to lead
successful social lives. Can you imagine a marriage, for instance, in
which the husband wears a tuxedo to breakfast every morning? We
have different relationships with different people—we rarely kiss
the boss good morning. The question is whether one's degree of

adaptation is so far ranging as to cause him psychological trauma.*
Our behavioral change in the presence of another is not necessarily
calculated like a stage play; it can be an honest adjustment to the
other's style. In a very honest sense, we are not the same to all people.
Different relationships conceal and reveal different aspects of our
personality [185].

We all have different roles or role identities which are prominent
at different times. Your adjustment to the demands of being a student
requires different behaviors than those expected during a long holi-
day at home. Based on a number of factors, the role identities are
called into prominence [185]. Based on the importance to you of a
given role, you do develop some consistency in your communication
behavior. Within a particular relationship, some consistency is
important or else no trust or enduring relationship can result. In fact,
when your actual behavior is consistent with yourself as you conceive it, then those communicating with you are also perceiving you
in that role. But when your behavior seems out of line with the role
others ascribe to you, others regard you as playing a game. A student
who has attended college and undergone dramatic changes in interests and lifestyle is often accused of "putting on airs" or being a
"smart college kid" upon returning home. His behavior is no longer
consistent with their images of him, and that is disrupting to them.

If you have a particular self-concept that does not fit with others'
expectations, your task is to convince others that your self-concept is
accurate. People who are successful in convincing others that how
they perceive themselves is accurate have been called self-confident,
autonomous, strong-willed, or persuasive. All of us have degrees of
conviction and strong will, yet still are affected by others' views. One
of the most dramatic attempts to assert independence from the roles
others assign for us is demonstrated in Frederick Perls' short poem:

I do my thing
and you do your thing.
I am not in this world
to live up to your expectations
And you are not in this world
to live up to mine.

---

*Rogers [234] and Sarbin and Allen [256] label this as "congruence." When
one's self-concept is consistent with the role demands, he is congruent.

> You are you
> and I am I
> and if by chance
> we find each other,
> it's beautiful.
> If not, it can't be helped.

In a sense, it is incorrect to talk about "hiding the self" or "staging a presentation." We do not have some *real self* that we can hide or reveal. We don't have some entity that we dress up and dress down for display. In a given situation, we have a set of behaviors that we consider to be (1) appropriate to the situation and (2) consistent, to some degree, with the self-concept we have. If we violate our expectations or personal desires too much, then we feel that we have played a game in that situation. Take the student, for example, who feels that he has received an unjust grade on his essay test. He sits up late at night outlining his arguments and rehearsing the defense he will make to the instructor. Just before entering the instructor's office, he wipes his sweaty brow, takes a deep breath, and then marches in. Once in the presence of the instructor, he is about one-fourth as self-assured, logical, and bombastic as he wanted to be. He is self-conscious, awed by the instructor's knowledge, and unable to hit hard verbally. The instructor, regretably, cannot be budged from his evaluation and the student returns home with the same grade. Was the student untrue to himself? Was he playing a game? No—he was simply adjusting to the presence of the instructor and setting forth appropriate behaviors. Even in more extreme cases, such as a job interview when an individual is consciously planning to present only the best aspects of himself, he is not violating any real self. He is simply selecting an appropriate repertoire of his possible behaviors.

The "looking-glass" self, the self built by social comparison, and the demands of our social roles are all interrelated. They are variations on the same theme—our self-concept is formed by our social relationships with others.

MAINTENANCE AND CHANGE OF SELF-CONCEPT

Having examined the components of the self-concept, and having noted that the self-concept arises and is sustained in our communicative transactions with others, we must take a more detailed look at the mechanisms used to maintain and change the self-concept. It was emphasized earlier that one's self-concept is a residue of past social encounters that one activates in each new transaction. The crucial question is, How does one maintain the self-concept at a somewhat uniform level if one continually engages in communicative trans-actions?

One's self-concept is maintained at reasonable levels because of *selectivity*. Selectivity takes many forms, all of which serve to give some stability to one's self-concept. In general, (1) we can selectively expose ourselves to individuals who support our self-concept, (2) we can selectively interpret either our or the other person's behavior, and (3) we can selectively choose the goals we wish to achieve [164, 238].

We selectively expose ourselves to individuals who support our self-concept. We choose certain people to associate with because they are the ones who think well of us. In a time of personal crisis, which is one of the situations that prompts self-awareness, we go to a friend because of the support we expect to obtain. Put bluntly, "friendship is the purest illustration of picking one's propaganda" [238]. Even on a day-to-day basis, our continuing transactions with our friends lend support to our self-concept. And quite clearly, the more people who attribute traits to you that you feel you possess, the more your self-concept will be resistant to change [2]. If your most personal dyadic contacts are with people who react to you in very stable ways, your self-concept will appear to be stable.

Selective interpretation of your own and other people's behavior is another mechanism that lends stability to your self-concept. When we are exposed to situations that can threaten our self-concept, we selectively interpret the information [277]. As Rosenberg says, "There is scarcely any behavior which cannot be interpreted as admirable in some way . . ." [238].* The operation of selective interpretation can be observed most vividly in individuals with high self-esteem. Such individuals tend to respond to a specific failure by evaluating themselves higher [106]. One of the most intriguing state-ments regarding the maintenance of the self-conception I have ever seen came from a poem written by a student in one of my classes. He wrote it in response to a guest lecture which stressed that too many of

---

*Hamachek [114] discusses extensively the self-defense mechanisms for-mulated by Freud.

us see ourselves as losers (frogs). Rather we should see ourselves as winners, or princes:

Frogs and Princes

Since we are here for only a short time
And while we're here we earn some dimes
These precious dimes may be many or few
It depends a lot on our personal views.

And if I'm a frog and you are a prince
And you have brains and I lack sense.
You will be a winner and I will lose,
But aren't most frogs faithful and true?

And suppose frogs are faithful and true,
Can't I as a frog become a winner, too?
And if a frog can win at this game
Who can say frogs and princes aren't really the same?*

The third major way one can selectively protect his level of self-concept is by a choice of goals. A person typically values those qualities and abilities in which he considers himself to excel and devalues those qualities in which he fails to excel. Further, he will selectively expose himself to situations in which he will excel [238]. The boy who did not make the basketball team may suddenly develop an interest in debate activities. The girl who is not invited to many social gatherings may develop a heightened interest in being a good student. The college professor who puts students to sleep in his classes may become more absorbed in his research activities. We all seek some degree of consistency between our goals and our degrees of success. After all, if you are five feet three inches tall and weigh one hundred pounds, it is rather foolish to continue getting smashed up in football when you have the option of selecting new goals.

The selectivity that we can exercise in order to maintain our self-concept does have its limits. Otherwise everyone would have a good self-concept which continually received support from other people. Circumstances are often such that we are restricted from having options from which to choose. Especially at an early age, one cannot choose who his parents will be or in what neighborhood he will live.

---

*Reprinted by permission of Stephen J. Wallace.

If the parents and friends disparage and reject him, a weakened self-concept is likely to result. Oftentimes too, choices are made that bring totally unexpected consequences for the self-concept. One can be placed in a situation where his talents and resources are not appropriate. The person starting a different job or the student attending a different college may experience a total lack of positive social support which obviously affects self-concept. We often do not realize the degree of dependence we have on other people until they are gone. One friend of mine experienced a precipitous decline in self-concept. She entered one social situation and for seven months experienced positive social support for her creativity and insight. She also became involved in a romantic dyad that was very meaningful to her. As a result of accepting a job in a new location, she had to change her residence. Much to her dismay, she discovered that she had no close friends nearby, her working associates did not provide the support to which she was accustomed, and she missed her romantic partner. During the months she remained there, her positive self-concept eroded to the point where the once self-assured, confident, friendly person became moody, depressed, and felt very inferior. After she returned to her previous place of residence and once again received a healthier dose of positive responses, her self-concept began the long climb to its previous level. While her experience is a bit more dramatic than most, it does demonstrate that the freedom to choose one's social support is sometimes limited.

If you desire to change your self-concept, for better or for worse, you might change environments and transact with different people. Cooley states that the chief advantage of travel and change is "to get away from one's working environment," which is, in a sense, "to get away from one's self . . ." [57]. As you enter a different social situation, because of the expectations and responses of others and the shifting, mutually adaptive, transactional nature of human behavior [123], your self-concept undergoes change. To go from rags to riches, or the reverse, will have a strong impact on how one sees oneself simply because the behavior of one's associates changes. The person who changes his way of life, whether he goes to college "to find himself" or changes jobs for "more stimulation," is really trying to match his talents with the expectations of others. The objective is to find people who appreciate you, for then you can appreciate yourself. Selectivity does have its limits, but if we can match our talents to the expectations of others, we will think better of ourselves.

An understanding of the process of forming the self-concept is essential for an accurate view of dyadic communication. The cyclic nature of self-conception, influencing and being influenced by our dyadic relationships, highlights the central role it plays in all transactions. As might be expected, there is a high correlation between self-regard and regard for others [294, 347], because the two are inextricably bound together in our social relationships. Furthermore, self-acceptance is essential for psychological growth and health [234]. Individuals who feel accepted, capable, and worthy are not those in mental hospitals and prisons; such places are peopled by those who feel unwanted and unaccepted. It is precisely those with a low self-concept that find it necessary to reject others. As Sullivan puts it, "it is not that as ye judge so shall ye be judged, but as you judge yourself so shall you judge others" [295]. Or in more negative terms, " . . .if you are a molehill, then, by God, there shall be no mountains" [296]. Thus the self-concept is a potent perception influencing your dyadic relationships.

SUMMARY

People have the ability to think about themselves and, as a result, develop self-concepts (generalized views of themselves). One's self-concept has multiple components and is basically social in nature. The prime determinants of one's self-concept are (1) the perceptions others have of him, (2) the comparisons he makes between himself and others, and (3) the social roles with which he is identified. While one's self-concept is shaped by communicative transactions with others, it also shapes those transactions. Self-concepts are an inextricable element of the transactional communication process—they influence and are influenced by each dyadic communication event. The residue from previous events comprises the self-concept that one brings to each new situation.

Selective exposure to others, selectively interpreting their behaviors, and selectively choosing goals are all methods of sustaining one's level of self-concept. While selectivity is a potent force tending to stabilize one's self-concept, there are limits. Whenever choices are restricted, or when one loses social support from others, it is difficult to maintain the previous level of self-concept.

Chapter 3
Perception of the Other

The process of perceiving the other person in a dyadic relationship serves the same function as does self-perception—it is another contributor to the meanings we assign to the situation [121]. And of course, the *meanings we assign determine our reactions.* We act toward others based upon the meanings we have for them [185].

This chapter treats the topic of person perception as it applies to dyadic transactions. While a vast literature has been compiled detailing the physiological aspects of perception, it is only dealt with in this chapter where it applies directly to communicative transactions. The focus for the chapter is on the perception of persons as an important element in dyadic transactions.

THE TRANSACTIONAL NATURE OF PERSON PERCEPTION

The psychologically naive individual operates under the assumption that he "perceives and observes other people in a correct, factual, unbiased way" [132]. If he perceives Sam as dishonest, that means for him that Sam *is* dishonest. Such an approach, while it makes "reality" easy to deal with, ignores the transactional nature of perception. Put bluntly, there is no objective world of persons. We each interpret others in different ways. To be sure, there is much agreement over evaluations. Two girls may both agree, after each had to fight her way home, that Sam is "handy with the hands." But what does it mean? Sam needs affection? Sam is a male chauvinist? Sam's mother rejected him? Sam is over-reacting because he's afraid of girls? Sam would make a bad husband? Sam would make a good husband? Just as we can never know the real or ultimate self, we cannot know what Sam is really like. We can say, however, that "this was my experience and this is how I react," recognizing that others experience a different aspect of Sam and attach their own meanings. The following anecdote best illustrates the point that our meaning for another's behavior is subject to error.

The small son of upper-class parents worried them considerably. In the presence of strangers, the boy stammered, withdrew, and became quiet. When around other children he became afraid and nervous. The parents felt the need to secure some professional help for the boy but wanted to do it so that the boy would not be embarrassed or feel singled out. Finally they hit upon an idea. An old college friend of the father was a clinical psychologist, so they invited him to dinner. After the meal, they revealed the real reason they had asked him over—to diagnose the son's problem. He accepted the task of observing the boy the next day (after, of course, collecting appropriate information on history and behavior).

He watched, unseen, from a balcony above the garden where the boy played by himself. The boy sat pensively in the sun, listening to neighboring children shout. He frowned, rolled over on his stomach, kicked the toes of his white shoes against the grass, sat up and looked at the stains. Then he saw an earthworm. He stretched it out on the flagstone, found a sharp-edged chip, and began to saw the worm in half. At this point, impressions were forming in the psychologist's mind, and he made some tentative notes to the effect: "Seems isolated and angry, perhaps over-aggressive, or sadistic, should be watched carefully when playing with other children, not have knives or pets." Then he noticed that the boy was talking to himself. He leaned forward and strained to catch the words. The boy finished the separation of the worm. His frown disappeared, and he said, "There. Now you have a friend" [262].

The transactional nature of person perception can also be understood by comparing it to object perception. When an object is perceived, the meaning attached to it is a function of (1) the perceiver, (2) the object, and (3) the situation. For purposes of illustration, look at Fig. 3–1 (Vernon, 1962).

•   •   •

•   •   •   •

Fig. 3–1   Arrangement of dots.

What do you see? Probably dots arranged in the forms of a triangle and a square. Look again! On the left are three dots and on the right are four dots. Why did they not produce the following shapes in your mind?

Or, why were they not seen as totally unrelated to one another? Clearly, what you perceived was as much a function of you as it was the arrangement of dots.

If the perception of objects is a "transaction between the brain and the environment" [219], the process of person perception is certainly no less a transaction. As a *minimum* in person perception, there is (1) the perceiver, (2) the person, and (3) the situation. In addition, some important elements are added in a dyadic relationship that are not present in the perception of objects. To begin with, there is a *mutually shared field* [303].* You see him and he sees you. The person you are perceiving is engaging in the same process you are. The complexity of the situation is best described by Tagiuri [301]:

> The perceiver, in some sense aware of many of the general properties of the other person (consciousness, mind) or his specific attributes (for example, generosity), has to allow for the fact that he himself, with similar properties, is also the object of perception and thought and that, as such, he influences his own object of perception. Observer and observed are simultaneously observed and observer. Their reciprocal feedback processes modify their self-presentation and, in turn, their reciprocal perceptions, in a continuous recycling but varying process during which each person uses the variations in himself and the other person as a means of validating his hypotheses about the other.

Your own behavior in a dyadic transaction produces reactions in the other, which you then use as the basis of your own perception. And the same process is occurring for the other participant. The process of person perception is obviously more complex than is object perception because the object is not adjusting to our presence. Often the conclusion that another person's behavior is consistent simply means that we provide a "self-picture which remains relatively stable and coherent," which has consistent effects on the other's behavior [99]. The personality characteristics which you perceive in a person may depend in part on the characteristics he perceives in you [176].

We can never perceive the "real" person because the concept of *the* "real" person is a myth. Another person's behavior is just as rela-

---

*Tagiuri calls this a double interaction, essentially a transaction.

tionship-bound as ours is. For example, if you perceive a person acting in a hostile manner, his perception of your behavior as hostile could have triggered his response. Furthermore, we often project onto others. We see things in them that are not in them, but are in us [132]. For instance, if you are feeling alone and bitter because of the recent loss of a romantic partner, you may tend to perceive other people as being lonely. And conversely, "when you're smiling, the whole world smiles with you."

At the very least, person perception is a transactional process because what we see is as much a function of us as it is of the qualities of the other person. For example, when you are really angry at someone, your reaction may say more about you than it does him.* There is no "immutable reality" [73] of the other person awaiting our discovery. Our perception of him will always be grounded in permanent uncertainty.

Research dealing with person perception, while often not giving appropriate emphasis to its transactional nature, has formulated some conclusions concerning the process. There are some general principles about the process we go through when attaching meaning to another's behavior, and they will be discussed under the topic of perceptual regularities. Two of the most important perceptual regularities occurring in dyadic contexts are (1) the imposition of structure and (2) the attribution of causality.

PERCEPTUAL REGULARITIES

Imposing Structure.   Just as we impose structure upon objects, such as seeing the dots of Fig. 3–1 in a pattern, we impose a structure upon a person's behavior. We always have to act on the basis of incomplete information, and we make sense of the incomplete information *by going beyond it* [44]. We take the initial and incomplete information and use it to define the person, to place him in a particular category. We do this because our world of experience has (1) structure, (2) some stability, and therefore (3) meaning [118a]. The Asch (1946)

---

*When someone is flying into a rage about something someone else has done and you are present, tell him, "That says more about you than it does him." It's usually good for a few minutes of reflection. This technique comes from John R. Wenburg.

study is one of the best examples of how we structure impressions of others based on partial information. Subjects were given a list of traits of an individual and were asked to write a paragraph describing the person. They also chose from a list of opposing traits those they felt characterized the person. Subjects formed overall impressions of persons based on such terse descriptions as intelligent, skillful, industrious, warm, determined, practical, and cautious. And furthermore, when the word warm was replaced by the word cold, impressions were considerably altered. Overall impressions of others are based on partial evidence; we translate the partial evidence, whether it comes from a list of words or a short transaction with the other, into a meaningful structure. Once we construct this model of the other, we guide our responses appropriately [187]. For instance, if you interpret a new acquaintance's acts as generally morose, you will then use this overall structure as the basis for your reactions.

The structure that we impose upon situations is uniquely ours. As Kelly [145] noted, we interpret information within the realm of our personal constructs. We "make sense" out of the other through our own personal experiences and ways of viewing the world [70]. In fact, the person's behavior is understandable to us *only to the extent that we can tie it back to our own experience* [324]—only to the extent that we have a construct for it. While the way each of us construes events is personal, there is enough commonality between two peoples' constructs to allow overlap in constructs [79]. Therefore, if you and Sally both observe Bob in the same situation, your interpretations of his behavior may have enough commonality that you "agree" on what you perceive to be his personality.

A related aspect of our imposition of structure is that we assume personal consistency on the part of others [99]. Because we attribute a "definiteness of attitudes, sentiments, and views" to others [132] when it is not there, we are often surprised. The young man who was a serious student shocks his parents by quitting his job and traveling alone around the world. The boy who was a juvenile delinquent suddenly breaks his habits and spends his next few years helping others. And the freewheeling, loose bachelor joins the monastery.

Oftentimes our expectation for consistency in others' behavior can produce humor. Joe was a semiserious student in one of my classes (he attended and participated, but did not study very hard). He was older than the other students, having reached the age of thirty, and was the father of four children. All in all, I saw him as a responsible, hard-working student. One day during a rather rigorous final examination, he was sitting in the back of the room and, like the other students, was intensely involved in the test. All of a sudden, when I looked his way his hand shot into the air with a huge middle finger extended—and a grin on his face. His gesture was so unexpected and so disruptive to my view of him that all I could do was laugh in front of a very puzzled class.

We often punish people who violate our conceptions of what they are. When we label someone's behavior as insincere or label him as a fake, we are only saying that he violated how we expect to perceive him. One study demonstrated that predictable people tend to be liked more than unpredictable ones [99]. Because (1) we want consistency in the other, (2) our behavior often produces consistency in the other's response, and (3) we impose consistent views of the other, we have a tendency to evaluate others in terms of particular personality traits [132]. If someone always acts intelligent around us, we tend to ascribe it as a personality trait that he carries with him to all other situations, when in fact it as well as all his other behaviors are situationally determined. The total mix of (1) your meaning and behavior and (2) his meaning and behavior produces the "personality" you perceive. There may be certain tendencies for response—he may wish to be a happy person—but the situation has to be appropriate in order to observe that quality in him.

Attributing Causality.   The second perceptual regularity characteristic of person perception is the attribution of causality. As human beings, we want to come to grips with our environment; we want to make sense out of the world. One of the techniques we utilize to this end is the attribution of causality. From the general view that events are caused, we view human behavior as being caused.* Most of us feel we are in part responsible for our actions, and we impose this same perspective on others. We see them as at least partly responsbile for their actions [301].

The degree of responsiblity we place on others for events depends on a number of factors. If external forces are not very strong

---

*This assumption, often stated in more esoteric terminology, underlies all physical and social scientific inquiry.

or if the ability to withstand those forces is regarded as high, we tend to place causality in the lap of the other. If the person has the ability to create effects, he is typically held responsible for those effects [300]. When observing a disintegrating marriage, for example, if we feel that one of the partners had it in his power to cause the demise of the marriage by cavorting around, we place the responsibility on him. Furthermore, if we see the person intending to gain the desired goal, we are more likely to assign responsibility to him.* In sum, people are held responsible for the effects they intend to create and for effects they have the ability to create [121].

The crux of the matter is that in analyzing social situations, we usually have two choices. We can ascribe the effects either to the person or to the environment. If we see another fail at a task, we can attribute it to a lack of ability, "a personal characteristic, or to the difficult task, an environmental factor" [121]. Whichever path we choose has consequences for our transactions. If, in the case above, we see the person as failing because of a lack of ability, we may concomitantly perceive him as a weak-willed, nonpowerful person. Our tendency will be to blame him and to take the "he-had-it-coming" attitude toward his misfortunes. If, on the other hand, we ascribe his failure to environmental causes ("Anyone would have failed at that.") then we will see him in a friendlier light and be sympathetic to his plight. A special form of attributing causes to environmental forces occurs in the case of unconscious motivation. If you see someone's behavior as caused by circumstances beyond his understanding and control ("He had a bad childhood and that is why he is insane."), you will absolve him of blame. Our courts of law recognize that environmental forces may be so overwhelming in some cases that the individual should not be tried. The important point to remember in attributing causality is this: Your notion of causality in a particular case will influence your behavior.

ACCURACY IN PERCEPTION

One's successful adjustment to his social world depends to some extent upon an accurate perception of others. Numerous research projects, when considered collectively, can lead us to some general

---

*This list is an adaptation from Hastorf, Schneider, and Polefka's [118a] conclusion summarizing research on attribution.

conclusions concerning (1) accuracy in judging emotions and attitudes, and (2) the socially based nature of accurate perceptions.

We humans respond to the behavior of another as if it were an index of his emotional state. From the time of Darwin, there has been an interest in deciphering the process of assessing emotions. While it is risky to draw any definite conclusions at this point [118a], we can say this: The more information you have about a situation, the more accurate your judgment will be. More information leads to less "filling in" on your part [79]. A grimace on someone's face can be interpreted in innumerable ways, but if you also see him attempting to lift a 200-pound weight, the meaning becomes clearer for you. Unfortunately most of the studies on perceptual accuracy have portrayed aspects of persons separated from a total context (such as having the picture of a face flashed on a screen). Not only do we know that we can more accurately recognize emotions in context, we know that the ability to recognize emotions is mostly developed through social experience. The ability to accurately perceive when someone is kidding you, for example, arises from your experience with kidding behavior in the past. Only the most basic emotional expressions are recognized through innate ability [301]; the rest are recognized as a result of cultural training.

The ability to accurately perceive another's attitudes increases with time. Altman and Taylor [6] specify that as a relationship develops, the participants share more and more central aspects of their orientations. Romantic pairs, for instance, typically go through "periods of adjustment" when one member is learning, often painfully, that the attitude of the partner is not what he (she) thought. In experimentally created dyads, initial awareness between partners is very low, although better than chance [304]. With continuing transactions, estimates of the other's attitudes typically improve [39, 304, 322]. It may well be that the most pronounced effect of transacting with another person is a heightened awareness of his attitudes when he is in your presence.

What factors produce an accurate estimate of the other's emotions or attitudes? Allport [5] suggests that personal characteristics such as extent of personal experience, intelligence, cognitive complexity, self-insight, and social skill may be related to the ability to accurately perceive another's emotions and attitudes. On the other hand, accuracy in judgment may simply be a matter of matching judges and subjects who are similar in attributes. For example, if they both have conventional attitudes, the degree of accuracy may be produced by the judge projecting his own attitudes and emotions into the other. It just so happens that they match.

Three response sets occur in person perception that affect its accuracy. In exercising judgments of others, people typically manifest (1) halo effects, (2) logical errors, and (3) leniency effects [301]. The halo effect operates when we observe certain characteristics and generalize about them. If George does his job quite well, most people will then assume he can also perform other tasks well. Closely related to this is the logical error, namely, the judge's conception of what goes with what—his system of categories. The constructs or categories you use may impel you to "put together" behaviors that may be distinct. Both of these errors relate closely to what we discussed in the opening pages of this chapter, namely, that one structures his experiences and supplies meanings that go beyond the data present. The leniency effect is rather fascinating in its own right. It is that we tend to judge people too high on favorable traits and too low on unfavorable traits. It may be that the operation of leniency in judgments is what sustains dyads in early phases of their transactions. When you have only limited information about the other person, it is not easy to reject him out of hand. As Rosenberg says, "Men living in society are thus under pressure to protect one another's self-esteem" [238]. Awareness of the leniency effect prompted someone to argue against it in the form of a wall plaque. It reads as follows:

Nobody Is Perfect

Each one of us is a mixture of good qualities and some perhaps not-so-good qualities. In considering our fellow-man, we should remember his good qualities and realize that his faults only prove that he is, after all, a human being.

We should refrain from making harsh judgments of a person just because he happens to be a dirty, rotten, no good son-of-a-__ __ __ __ __.

While the above conclusions concerning the accuracy of person perception can be made, their application to our own dyadic relationships is not an easy task. Unlike a rigorously devised experiment, there are often no standards in our dyadic relationships that we can check to determine the accuracy of our perceptions. As with the case in building self-concept, the bases for comparing our person perceptions are social in nature. Our social reality, namely, the judgments of others around us, is our only guide to the "correctness" of our view of someone. All in all, the process of perceiving our dyadic partner is slippery business—not only will our own behavior affect his, but the only standards for comparison we have are the perceptions others have of him. And their perceptions are subject to the same limitations.

INTERPERSONAL ATTRACTION

It has been stressed repeatedly that the process of person perception is essentially the attachment of meaning to another's behavior. The meaning we attach to another's behavior takes many forms depending on the type of relationship. For romantic pairs the meaning each has for the other's behavior carries sexual connotations; for a teacher-pupil dyad the transaction may be based on mutual respect; while for an aider-aided dyad, such as a doctor and patient, the central meaning in the transaction may revolve around the need for a service. In all types of dyadic pairs, however, the attraction between the two people is a force central to their perceptions of each other. We all experience degrees of attraction toward others—there are some people we enjoy being around and others that, for some reason, we find repelling.

The basic degrees of feelings ranging between liking and disliking another—the degrees of attraction—are produced by a host of factors. Tagiuri [300] and Lindzey and Byrne [47, 48] have cataloged many of the factors that influence the attraction people feel toward others. The present section will highlight propinquity, similarity between participants, and the behavior one engages in as inextricably tied to the attraction one feels toward another.

Propinquity. Propinquity simply means proximity or physical closeness. The physical closeness of two persons has a dramatic impact on the attraction between them. The close geographical placement of two individuals allows a transaction to occur and sentiment or attraction to intensify.

Propinquity is one of the most crucial determiners in the formation of friendships. Close friendships are formed by being close. The classic Festinger, Schachter, and Back [88] study perhaps most clearly demonstrates the pronounced effects of physical proximity on friendship. They studied friendship development in a new housing project. A series of small houses formed a U-shaped court and some houses faced inward to an open grassy area while the end houses faced outward. Friendships were most affected by the distance between houses and the direction the houses faced. As the distance between houses increased, fewer friendships formed. The effects were so marked that it was rare to find friendships forming between individuals separated by more than four or five houses. Furthermore, those individuals who by chance happened to occupy the houses that faced outward had less than half as many friends in the project than did those whose houses faced inward.

In order for friendship to result, some activity has to provide a setting for contact to occur. In the author's own neighborhood, the effects of the seasons significantly alter friendships. During the winter my neighbor across the street keeps his car in his garage behind the house. As a consequence, the usual chit-chat and the "Hey, come on over for a drink!" atmosphere of the summer disappears. Likewise my friendship with the person across the alley from me wanes in the winter. During the summer we see each other in our gardens (His is much better than mine!) and talk for long periods of time. But carrot and tomato talk totally disappears in the winter, and we see each other only about once a month. Your own friendships probably developed because a job, hobby, or living area placed you in the proximity of the other people. Friendship develops from transacting with others and conversations are often started between those that share an activity that places them in close physical proximity.

Not only are friendship pairs affected by propinquity, the selection of a romantic partner is heavily influenced by it. A large proportion of marriages are between people who reside close to each other [29]. Numerous studies have demonstrated that the closer two potential marital partners live, the better is the probability of a marriage occurring. If the building is designed to promote transactions, the bachelor and bachelorette who move into an apartment complex to find a mate are making a wise choice. You have to meet someone before a romantic relationship can form, and physical proximity provides the opportunity. Even extramarital romantic liaisons are greatly affected by propinquity. The boss-secretary relationship, for instance, is a classic one. This type of relationship has the opportunity to develop because the participants work in close relation to each other.

Why doesn't proximity also produce intense dislike? Sometimes it does, but it usually produces the opposite. Of course, if a group of people are forced so close together that they hardly have room to breathe, proximity can work against close friendship. When two fur trappers are penned into their small cabin for two months by the winter snow they get cabin fever, but such cases happen rather infrequently. For most of us, carrying out routine activities in close proximity to another produces some degree of fondness. Newcomb [210] noted that with close contact comes more information, usually favorable, about the other. Since we typically are concerned with others and they with us in a transaction, it is reasonable that such attraction is formed. This mutuality of rewarding each other produces positive sentiment [130].

Seen from another point of view, a transaction with another often gives us the feeling of being included. Since inclusion is a basic human need [267], it follows that the satisfaction of a need produces pleasure and therefore liking. In any event, proximity has a tendency to produce liking more than disliking. However, a specific prediction of the effects of proximity on any two dyadic participants would be risky. In order to predict whether two particular individuals thrown into proximity will form a friendship or romantic pair would require an amazing amount of information. You would have to know their backgrounds, needs, past transactions, meanings they assign to others, and self-concepts—and these are only a few of the crucial elements. We will have to be satisfied at this point with a very general conclusion: Propinquity allows friendships and romances the opportunity to flourish.

In conclusion, the following anecdote demonstrates an interesting case of propinquity producing sexual attraction. A graduate student has boarded a bus for a long, weary ride home:

> After an hour or so, the bus stopped in a small town, and a few passengers got on. One of them was a blonde girl, very good looking in a fresh but sort of sleazy way. I thought that she was

probably a farm girl, and I wished she'd sit by me. By God, she did. She was really comely, if you know what I mean, and she smiled a bit so I felt sure she'd be approachable. Oh, boy, what luck. I didn't want to be too eager, and I was still exhausted, so we just smiled and talked for a minute. I made sure that she was comfortable, and then sort of dozed off for a little while, hoping to recuperate by the time the driver turned out the lights and meanwhile enjoying my fantasies about the prospects for the rest of the trip. The last thing I remember was smiling at her and noticing that when her skirt slipped up on her knee as she reached up to the back of the seat, she didn't pull it down. Wow! About four hours later we were pounding along the road in complete darkness when I opened my eyes. Her leg, the outside of it, was against mine, and the way it pressed and moved with the motion of the bus woke me up. This was more than I'd dreamed of. I was terribly excited, and when I stirred a little the steady pressure of her leg didn't move away. By this time, I had a terrific erection, and the more I thought about this cute little babe pressing against me, the worse it got. I was just about to reach out and touch her when we pulled into a gas station for a stop, and when the light came through the window, *she* wasn't there at all! She must have left while I was asleep. A fat man with a growth of beard and a dead cigar dropping ash on his vest was sprawled next to me, sound asleep. It was *his* leg pressing against me, and he was so fat and slovenly that even when I drew myself away, his sloppy flesh stayed against me. I was so dumbfounded—disappointed, too, and the funny thing—I lost that erection almost immediately, got up and moved to another seat. What a let down [262].

Similarity.   Interpersonal attraction is not only affected by propinquity; as two individuals begin to interact, a host of other factors influences their mutual attraction. One of these factors, similarity, has been extensively investigated.

Do birds of a feather flock together? Or do opposites attract? A number of studies have shown that if the birds are lovebirds and human, then those flocking together do tend to be of like feather. Byrne's review of literature led him to the conclusion that ". . . the association between similarity and attraction has consistently been verified in the husband-wife studies" [48]. The similarity was attitudinal; marital partners tended to agree with each other about topics ranging from communism to birth control. Furthermore, friendship pairs show the same type of similarity of attitude patterns [46]. Therefore, for marital and friendship dyads, there is an association between attitude similarity and attraction [48].

Why should similarity and attraction be related? Duck [79] has demonstrated that friends have similar personal constructs and, in addition, they are aware of the similarity. The similarity leads to attraction because ". . . cognitive similarity leads to communication effectiveness, communication effectiveness leads to rewards, and these to interpersonal attraction" [305]. It does seem reasonable that as we communicate effectively with another, our attraction is built because a successful transaction is rewarding, and we like those who reward us [29].

The relationship between similarity and attraction can be seen in reverse by specifying that attraction produces similarity. One of the things that happens is that as individuals interact, each selects objects of common interest that highlight agreement [211]. And of course, it may be that we select people to interact with that we see have some potential for agreement. According to the balance theory, [121] we strive to make sense out of our relationships. If we see ourselves as similar to someone else, we expect to like him. Furthermore, if we dislike someone we expect to have dissimilar attitudes on important issues.

Dyadic participants often overestimate the similarity between their attitudes. Levinger and Breedlove's [167] study, for example, showed that husbands and wives tended to be similar in some attitudes, but the assumed similarity was higher than the actual similarity. Spouses typically overestimate their attitudinal agreement [49], and yet this overestimation has desirable consequences. When one overrates his similarity to his spouse, and vice versa, rewards are increased [48]. We are rewarded by others when we agree with them, and it is certainly easier to receive those rewards by misperceiving the other's attitude than to change one's own [49].

While interpersonal attraction is closely associated with attitude similarity, it is not necessarily related to other types of similarity. For instance, romantic partners are not necessarily similar in social desirability. At the early stages of a relationship, "it appears that everyone prefers the most attractive date possible" [29]. Attraction to a romantic partner is not contingent upon similarity of social standing. One word of optimism to those who are not seen as socially desirable, and a word of caution to those who have a date every night—while perceived physical attractiveness is a prime factor in dating choice, it is not in the selection of marital partners [79].

One area of similarity that has been little explored has to do with communication style. For example, are we attracted to people who have communicating styles similar to ours? Do talkers like fellow talkers or are they in search of listeners? Are impulsive people frustrated by working with individusls who make very deliberate decisions? Such issues are of crucial importance if we are to understand the process of mutual attraction between people. A second area in need of exploration is the type of attraction between two individuals. We can like people on entirely different bases. You may be attracted to one person because of his ability to liven up a party, to another because of his deep thoughts, and to a third because of his physique. To expect to find some similarity between you and all of them (compared to the things in which you are dissimilar) is asking a bit too much. Hendrick [125] demonstrated, for example, that most people choose extroverts when choosing leaders and those who would be interesting at a party. The demands of each particular social relationship influence which qualities we will perceive as desirable. Few of us would select an exact replica of ourselves as a friend, nor would we choose an opposite with whom we had absolutely nothing in common [219].

Behavior.   Your *own* behavior greatly influences the perception you have of another person. In one study, the attraction people had for others was a consequence of their own behavior [264]. For example, if you perform a favor for another you tend to like him better as a result [140]. Another experiment found that subjects who read negative evaluations to another (and did not anticipate meeting that person afterwards) changed their impressions in a negative way [67]. In the Glass study, subjects with high self-esteem who acted out some aggressive behavior toward another person came to dislike their victim [101]. In these cases, the evaluation of the other changes in order for it to be consistent with one's behavior. If you voluntarily treat another as if you like him, your liking for him will increase; if you treat him poorly, you will tend to dislike him more.

The fact that perception of others is influenced by your own behavior underscores the transactional nature of person perception. Obviously, the process of person perception is "even more complex than one ever dreamt" [301]. It is complex because all the elements of the process are related:

1. Perception leads to evaluation and evaluation leads to perception [121].

2. Similarity leads to interpersonal attraction; interpersonal attraction leads to similarity (see above).

3. Perception of yourself and perception of others are highly related and part of a cyclic process (see Chapter 2).

4. Transacting with another leads to positive sentiment; positive sentiment toward another leads to transactions with him [130].

The work on person perception has not typically focused on a transactional point of view. Few pieces of research have attempted to look at such perception as a joint process of both the perceiver and the perceived. Furthermore, instead of concurrently looking at A's perception of B and B's perception of A, most of the studies have focused on only half of the process. As Hastorf, Schneider, and Polefka note, "We need to know more about how people get to know one another; such knowledge would entail the matching of one person's perception of another with the other's perception of himself" [118a]. We would obviously be concerned with more aspects than that, but the point is clear. We should look at the process of coordination of meaning between communication participants—at their joint perceptions of each other. When this is done, our understanding of dyadic transactions will be strengthened.

SUMMARY

One of the central parameters of dyadic communication is the process of person perception. When another person is perceived, the perceiver (1) imposes structure on available cues, (2) attributes causality to events, and (3) typically commits errors in accuracy.

These perceptual regularities mean that person perception is a transactional process. What one perceives another to be is a function of the available cues, the situation, and the perceiver himself. The perceiver is part of the very situation he is perceiving. His own behavior can influence his perception of the other—for example, if he performs a favor for the other, he will like the other better. In addition, the perceiver's behavior affects the behavior of the other, which in turn affects the perceiver's perception of the other.

Research on person perception should focus more on the cyclic, mutually influencing nature of person perception in dyads.

Part II
Relationships: The Key to Transactions

Chapter 4
The Nature of Dyadic Relationships

I SEE YOU SEEING ME

You are sitting alone in the library and are watching a young man who comes in, selects a table twenty feet from yours, and settles down. Then, just as you are beginning to stare at him, he looks back. You are caught, are somewhat embarrassed, and try to pretend that you were not really looking. You try to deny that a relationship has been formed.

Experiences such as this demonstrate that a relationship between two people is something uniquely different from the act of one person observing another. Dyadic communication does not occur simply because two people are placed near each other. The participants have to recognize that they have formed a *relationship* before a dyadic system is fully operable. A relationship is formed when the following elements are present:

1. You and another are behaving.
2. You are aware of his behavior, and, at the same time,
3. He is aware of your behavior.
4. As a result,
    a) you are aware that he is aware of you.
    b) he is aware that you are aware of him.

Put simply, a person is aware that he is in a dyadic relationship when he has the *perception of being perceived* [246]. When both persons can say, "I see you seeing me," then an interpersonal bond has been formed because of their reciprocal awareness.

When you enter into a dyadic relationship, the world is no longer exclusively your own. The other person has to be considered. You have to adjust to his presence and he to yours because each transaction you enter entails segments of commitment and adjustment. Each person is a full participant in the transaction; no one is strictly an observer, nor strictly the observed. Each person's perceptions influence the relationship because each participant affects and is affected by the other. Put another way, once you have entered into a relationship, a system has been formed in which there is no such thing as isolated behavior.

THE COMMUNICATION SYSTEM

A dyadic transaction can be described as having the qualities of an open system. Once a relationship is formed the system has been activated, and once in process it has certain qualities. Some of the most important qualities of a dyadic communication system are (1) wholeness, (2) synergy, (3) circularity, and (4) equifinality [330].

Wholeness occurs whenever all the elements of a system are interrelated. Such is the case with dyadic communication. When a change occurs in one participant, its effects reverberate throughout the system. For example, take the case of the dyadic transactions between a wife and husband. The two of them form a unique system based on their relationship, in this case characterized by the wife raising the children and staying at home. If she undergoes a change in her aspirations and wants to launch a career of her own, the wife-husband relationship will be altered. Their relationship cannot stay the same if one of the partners undergoes change. In any ongoing dyadic transaction, any change in one part of the system affects other parts.

Dyadic communication is also characterized by synergy. Synergy means that the whole is greater than the parts, that $1 + 1 = 3$ [214]. The combined efforts of two people produce a greater effect than the sum of their individual actions. Putting two people together in a dyadic relationship creates a system that is composed of (1) person A, (2) person B, and (3) the ways A and B operate in relation to each other. Obviously, once in a relationship, the two begin mutually influencing each other, thereby creating effects that would not have occurred if the two were separated. Take the case of two young boys. They enter into a relationship and begin talking about stealing. Pretty soon, each boy is daring the other to steal some food from the local grocery store. While they are being escorted home by the store manager, each boy blames the other. Each boy is aware that he would not have gotten into trouble if he had been alone. The combined effects of dares and counterdares produced effects that would not have arisen had the boys not been together.

The effects of synergy also can be positive. In a romantic dyad, for example, the love and warmth generated in the system can reach quite intense levels. As one partner responds with open affection, it stimulates an openness and warmth in the other—which cycles back and produces more love in the other. Two "starry-eyed" lovers are a pleasant reminder that all dyadic relationships have synergy.

Circularity and feedback also characterize dyadic communication systems. The processes of influence are circular; everything influences everything else. Each participant is engaging in behavior and simultaneously monitoring the other person. Each person watches the other and responds to the other's response to him. Stated another way, each dyadic process is an uninterrupted sequence of interchanges [330].

The usual way of thinking about communication does not encompass the circularity point of view. If a romantic pair is involved in a conflict, each participant tends to assess causes and effects. Mary says, "John just doesn't treat me with respect and that's why we fight." Meanwhile John is analyzing their dyad and saying, "If Mary were not so domineering, we would get along fine." Both Mary and John are "punctuating"—stopping an ongoing circular process and labeling one behavior a cause and another as an effect. The truth is probably somewhere in the middle. Mary and John are both right and both wrong. By not realizing that each person's behavior is both a cause and an effect, they will probably not arrive at a successful resolution to their conflict. Mary could change her behavior (or John could) and break the cycle they are caught up in. If Mary would stop acting in a domineering way, then John could respect her. And if John would respect her, Mary could stop acting in a domineering way. The processes of dyadic communication are indeed circular.

One other quality of any open system applies to the description of dyadic communication: equifinality [242]. Equifinality means that in an open system, the same state can be reached in different ways and from different beginning conditions. For instance, take a romantic pair that can be described as having a relationship based on self-respect, concern for the other, and open love. This same state can be reached in numerous ways. The pair could have met in Yellowstone National Park and only known each other for six weeks before marriage. Or they could have been childhood sweethearts and continued as a dyad until marriage, never having loved anyone else. It doesn't matter. The same state of an excellent romantic relationship can be arrived at from different directions. Communication viewed as an open system is a set of processes that are continually changing and adapting.

Since dyadic communication is a transactional process which has the attributes of an open system, it is *relational in nature*. To accurately capture the essence of any dyadic transaction, one must focus on the *relationship* between the participants. The proper study of dyadic communication is not limited to a study of each individual's psychology, because each personality comes into existence only in a relationship [243]. The proper study of dyadic communication, therefore, is the *pattern of relationships* between individuals. The remainder of this chapter will examine some relationship-based approaches to dyadic communication, highlight the formation and dimensions of relationships, and conclude by discussing the dyadic norm of reciprocity.

RELATIONAL FUNDAMENTALS

The Coorientation Model.   The work of Theodore Newcomb [209, 210] provides a starting point for a relational analysis of dyadic communication. His system consists of two individuals, A and B, and their orientation toward some object X. Each individual is cooriented—he has an orientation toward the other person and toward the object. Take A, for instance. He will have an orientation toward B (his attraction to B) and an orientation toward object X (his attitude toward object X). Communication performs the necessary function of enabling both A and B to "maintain simultaneous orientation toward one another and toward the object of communication" [209].

A friendship dyad can be used for illustration. A is Joe, B is Sam, and object X is snowmobiles. Figure 4–1 outlines the essentials of the system.

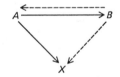

Fig. 4–1   The coorientation model.

The *minimal* components of this (or any) dyadic system from Newcomb's point of view are the following.

1. *A*'s attitude toward object *X*.
2. *A*'s attraction to *B*.
3. *B*'s attitude toward object *X*.
4. *B*'s attraction to *A*.

In this case, Joe dislikes snowmobiles and is attracted to Sam. Sam likes to snowmobile (he owns an $1800 machine) and considers himself a close friend of Joe. Each person has a coorientation, an attitude toward object *X* and an attraction toward the other person. With these minimal components, Newcomb postulates what he calls a "strain toward symmetry." If the object is important to us and we are attracted to another person, we expect them to also like the object. Strain develops because of a perceived discrepancy between *A*'s orientations to object *X* and what he perceives *B*'s orientations to be.* From Joe's point of view, if he likes Sam and dislikes snowmobiles, but Sam loves to snowmobile, then there is a strain on the system. Joe is an avid cross-country skier, and when skiing he is bothered by the noise of snowmobiles roaring past. Yet he is a close friend of Sam. The system is not balanced, and Joe will have to reconcile the strain by some action. Some of the alternatives he has are to (1) decrease his liking for Sam, (2) reduce the importance or relevance of snowmobiling by changing his attitude, or (3) communicate to Sam in order to change Sam's attitude.

Newcomb's analysis sets the building blocks for a relational approach to studying any dyadic pair. Joe, just like people in other dyads, does not function in a vacuum. His actions are dependent on both his own orientations and his perceptions of Sam's orientations. And Joe's orientations are influenced by his perceptions of the other's orientations. When we are in dyadic relationships, we have perceptions of what the other is thinking and the other has perceptions of what we are thinking.

This basic assumption—that each person (1) knows what he thinks and (2) has some estimate of what the other person thinks—

---

*This cursory treatment omits many details. The degree of felt strain is a function of the degree of perceived discrepancy, the degree of attraction to the other, and the importance and relevance of the object (snowmobiles). For more details, see Newcomb [209].

has been expanded by a more comprehensive look at coorientation [53, 54, 192, 302].* The expanded version of coorientation adds three key terms: agreement, congruence, and accuracy.

Agreement occurs when person A and person B have the same orientation toward the object X (see Fig. 4–2). Joe and Sam, for example, have a disagreement concerning snowmobiling. Obviously, evaluations of the object can range anywhere between agreement and disagreement. The more the disagreement or discrepancy between the two persons' evaluations, the greater the strain on the system.

Fig. 4–2   Assessing agreement in the coorientation model.

The coorientation model also incorporates what each person perceives the other's evaluations to be. Person A, for instance, has an orientation toward object X and an orientation toward person B. His orientation toward B incorporates his perception of what B thinks. If Joe liked snowmobiles and also thought Sam liked them, the system could be characterized by congruence I (Fig. 4–3). Similarly, congruence II is the same process of comparison from Sam's viewpoint.

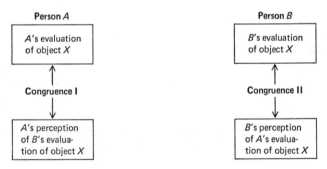

Fig. 4–3   Assessing congruence in the coorientation model.

---

*Tagiuri, et al. labeled accuracy, congruency, and mutuality of feelings as the three components. Mutuality of feelings is identical to agreement, and the term agreement will be used in this discussion. The figures are slight adaptations from Chaffee and McLeod [53].

Congruence occurs when A's estimate of B's evaluation of object X is the same as A's evaluation of object X.

A more complete picture of the elements of relationship between a dyadic pair is shown in Fig. 4–4. Accuracy I comes from comparing A's estimate of B's evaluation with B's actual evaluation of object X. If Joe correctly perceives Sam's opinion of snowmobiles, his estimate has been accurate. The identical comparisons, when made from Sam's perceptions, constitute accuracy II.

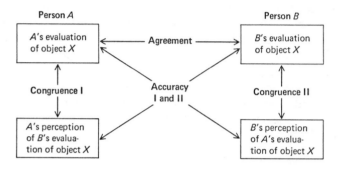

Fig. 4-4   Assessing agreement, congruence, and accuracy in the coorientation model.

Chaffee and McLeod [53] used the expanded coorientation model to demonstrate that panel designs produce sensitization in subjects. When subjects knew that other subjects were being tested on the same issue, they tended to focus on the other subject's opinions. Similarly, *individuals involved in a relationship make estimates of one another's orientations.* Joe's own opinion and actions regarding snowmobiles are affected in part by his perception of Sam's feelings. If Joe and Sam are exceptionally good friends, then Joe's appreciation and evaluation of snowmobiles may undergo significant changes (and so could Sam's).*

The coorientation model can be fruitfully applied to dyadic communication because it provides the groundwork for a relational analysis. Rather than observing two individuals as separate entities who just happen to communicate, we can begin to examine the rela-

---

*The earlier treatment of self-concept (Chapter 2) makes the same point. We develop our self-concept based on our estimates of what others think of us.

tionship itself. At a minimum, therefore, any index of a dyadic relationship should encompass (1) what each person's orientations are (attitude toward the object and attraction toward the other person) and (2) what each person perceives the orientations of the other to be. Such an approach would yield relational data such as congruence and accuracy. Such assessments are the *joint product* of the participants and not just the index of the perceptions of one person.

Like the coorientation model, any approach that centers on the *interpenetration of perspectives* of participants would qualify as a relational approach [258]. Drewery's [78] interpersonal perception technique, for example, focuses on how one person "perceives another and expects to be perceived" by him. Drewery analyzed a marital relationship from the standpoint of the mismatched perspectives of the participants, and even though a divorce resulted anyway, the method does show some promise for providing insight into dyadic processes. Ichheiser [132] mentions that a sociopsychological model of human relationships would include:

1. What we actually are.
2. What we think we are.
3. What other people think we are.
4. What we assume other people think we are (p. 150).

When one assesses items three and four for both participants, relational assessments can then be made. Whatever technique is chosen, the proper study and understanding of dyadic transactions are *at the relationship level.*

The Interpersonal Perception Method. While Ichheiser just mentions the relational approach, Laing, Phillipson, and Lee [160] deal specifically with the interperceptions and interexperience of the participants in a dyad. They take as a fundamental postulate that "the world is peopled by others, and these others are not simply objects in the world: they are centers of reorientation to the objective universe." For each individual two aspects are related, namely, one's own behavior and the other's experience of that behavior. When Peter engages in behavior, Paul can react only in terms of his experience of that behavior. The meaning that Paul attaches to Peter's behavior in turn influences Paul's behavior. *The behavior of each toward the* *other is mediated by the experience each has of the other.* Clearly Laing, Phillipson, and Lee see two participants in a transaction mutually affecting each other. In fact they state, "The failure to see the behavior of one person as a function of the behavior of the other has led to some extraordinary perceptual and conceptual abberations that are still with us" [160].

The interpersonal perception method was offered as a technique to relationally analyze dyads. Each participant has three perspectives that can be assessed. In the case of a romantic dyad, they are described as follows:

Husband's view of object X	Direct perspective
Husband's view of wife's view of object X	Metaperspective
Husband's view of wife's view of his view of object X	Meta-metaperspective

Similarly, the perspectives assessed from the wife would be:

Wife's view of object X	Direct perspective
Wife's view of husband's view of object X	Metaperspective
Wife's view of husband's view of her view of object X	Meta-metaperspective

Dyads utilize such perspectives, and Laing, et al. try to heighten our awareness of that process. For example, the perspectives of participants in a romantic dyad could be classified as follows:

He—"I sure do like sex."	(his direct perspective)
He—"She likes sex."	(his metaperspective)
He—"She thinks I like sex."	(his meta-metaperspective)
She—"I don't like sex."	(her direct perspective)
She—"He likes sex."	(her metaperspective)
She—"He thinks I like sex."	(her meta-metaperspective)

It's quite apparent that a serious relationship based on these perspectives will have some areas of conflict. The degree of overlapping or matching of perspectives is crucial for any dyadic encounter. Laing, Phillipson, and Lee suggest that the following relational aspects are helpful in understanding dyads:

1. Comparison between one person's direct perspective and the other person's direct perspective on the same issue yields *agreement* or *disagreement*.

2. Comparison between one person's metaperspective and the other person's direct perspective on the same issue yields *understanding* or *misunderstanding*.

3. Comparison between one person's meta-metaperspective and his own direct perspective yields the *feeling* of *being understood* or of *being misunderstood*.

4. Comparison between one person's meta-metaperspective and the other person's metaperspective on the same issue yields *realization* or *failure of realization*.

Using the sample case of the romantic pair, we can observe the operation of each of these relational statements. Figure 4–5 outlines the comparison of participant perspectives.

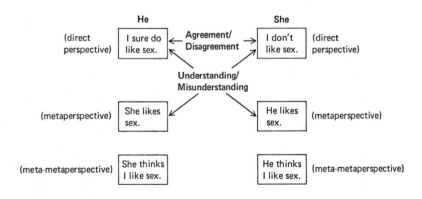

Fig. 4–5 Degrees of agreement and understanding with the interpersonal perception method.

The example demonstrates that the direct perspectives do not agree in this case. She correctly perceives that he likes sex, so she understands him on this issue (her metaperspective matches his direct perspective). Note, however, that he does not understand her on the sex issue (His metaperspective, "She likes sex," does not match her direct perspective.) This case could easily have been as follows: He and she could disagree about object X, sex, yet still understand each other.

Figure 4–6 completes the analysis. Here the feeling of being understood or misunderstood and the realization or failure of realization are sketched. If you were she, you would feel misunderstood because what you thought (direct perspective) and what you thought he thought you thought (meta-metaperspective) do not match. On the other hand, his direct and meta-metaperspectives match, so he feels understood.

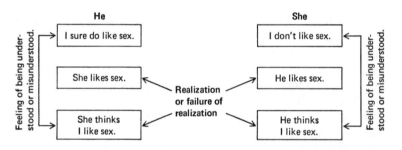

Fig. 4–6 Degrees of realization and feeling understood with the interpersonal perception method.

Realization means that a participant realizes the other person understands or misunderstands him. In this case, he realizes that she understands him. Correspondingly, she realizes that he misunderstands her. In each case, realization can be seen as follows: When he becomes aware of her metaperspective ("He likes sex"), he then can compare that to what he thinks she thought about his sexual tastes ("She thinks I like sex"). The comparison of the two allows him to realize that she understands him. The corresponding process can be followed for she, too.

The interpersonal perception method highlights the fact that relationships can be maintained on any number of bases. For instance, the participants may agree on an issue, yet one or both misunderstand each other. Or as we saw in Chapter 3 (Perception of the Other), the participants in a marital dyad may overestimate their similarity on issues. They may misunderstand each other and as a result think there is agreement when it is not present. The possible combinations of all the relational aspects are numerous. For instance, when there is agreement on an issue, there are four possible configurations of understanding:

1. He understands her; she understands him.
2. He understands her; she misunderstands him.
3. He misunderstands her; she understands him.
4. He misunderstands her; she misunderstands him.

When (1) the feeling of being understood or misunderstood and (2) the realization of failure of realization are added in, the complexity of dyadic relationships becomes apparent. It is yet to be determined what particular configurations of relational dimensions are most functional for a particular dyad. The most straightforward configuration is obvious—when there is agreement, understanding, the feeling of being understood, and realization on the part of both participants. It may be, however, that other configurations are more functional for particular dyads. For instance in a marital dyad, agreement on direct perspectives may be less important on crucial issues than is understanding. The participants may "agree to disagree" on some items as long as they understand each other's position. Whatever the relational configuration, the important element is how the participants respond to the relationship.

The coorientation model sketched earlier in Fig. 4–4 bears some similarity to the interpersonal perception method. The coorientation model assesses (1) A's and B's direct perspectives and (2) A's and B's metaperspectives. In terms of person A and person B, each system of analysis offers terms to classify relational aspects of the dyad (see Fig. 4–7).

There are, at least at the lower levels of relationship analysis, some direct parallels between the two methods.

The major difference between the two approaches is highlighted by noting that the IPM method takes into account higher and more complex levels of analysis. As a result, while Newcomb's original "strain toward symmetry" places the primary emphasis on agreement, IPM considers other relational options. In working with marital dyads, Laing demonstrated that even when couples could not reach agreement, if they increased their awareness of the other's attitudes, they were able to "work on their disagreements more effectively at those levels of perspective" [160]. Put simply, a couple can improve their relationship by relating more realistically, even without necessarily reaching overt agreement.

Point of comparison	Coorientation model	Interpersonal perception method
1. *A*'s direct–*B*'s direct	Agreement	Agreement/ Disagreement
2. *A*'s direct–*B*'s meta *B*'s direct–*A*'s meta	Accuracy	Understanding/ Misunderstanding
3. *A*'s direct–*A*'s meta *B*'s direct–*B*'s meta	Congruence	
4. *A*'s direct–*A*'s meta-meta *B*'s direct–*B*'s meta-meta		Feeling of being understood or misunderstood
5. *A*'s meta-meta–*B*'s meta *B*'s meta-meta–*A*'s meta		Realization or failure of realization

Fig. 4–7   Comparison of coorientation and interpersonal perception method models.

This discussion of the coorientation model and the interpersonal perception method has, of necessity, been detailed. In spite of their differences, the two methods provide *relationship approaches* to dyadic communication. The irreducible unit of analysis becomes the *comparison across participant perspectives.*

Some applications of a relationship approach have been available for some time. For example, Dymond [80] studied the phenomenon of empathy by essentially comparing the direct perspectives and metaperspectives of two people. Tagiuri [299], in studying sociometric choice, also asked participants, "Who do you think he will choose?"—an example of a metaperspective. Drewery's recent work and that of Laing, Phillipson, and Lee demonstrate that marital dyads can be studied from such vantage points. The latter authors found, for example, that disturbed marriages, when compared to nondisturbed marriages, manifest more disagreement and more misunderstanding. While such results certainly are not conclusive, they are highly suggestive that a relational approach to dyadic transactions can be very useful.*

THE NEGOTIATION OF SOCIAL IDENTITIES

When two people are mutually aware of each other, and when each is aware of the other's awareness, a relationship has been formed. But stating that a relationship has been formed is only the beginning of an ongoing relationship. Relationships differ according to the kinds of adjustments participants make to each other's presence.

The key to a relationship building and sustaining communication behavior is how each participant adjusts to the other. The two individuals' behavior has to be coordinated in some ways for a successful transaction to occur. If the persons act totally independent of each other, as do some schizophrenics and small children, then no transaction—the coordination between two individuals—can occur [9]. For instance, a young child usually has difficulty entering into another's point of view, is egocentric, and believes his own judgments to be absolute [226]. It is not until the child discovers that other points of view are possible and that reality is what is common by all points of view taken together that he can form relationships. Relationships demand that each participant (1) have his own definition of the situation and (2) be aware of, and adjust to, how he thinks the other person defines the relationship (metaperspective).

One inescapable element present in the mutual definition of any relationship is *role*. In fact it can be said that "in a relationship we are always in roles, by definition" [243]. The role you see yourself in

---

*There are some ambiguities in the method used by Laing, et al. For instance, in studying marital dyads, a question on direct perspective is as follows: How true to you think the following is? "She understands me." It appears that in assessing a direct perspective on the object X of "She understands me," the authors are already asking for a metaperspective. Basically in this case, the object X is a relational statement.

places a boundary on the relationship. If you perceive yourself as an employee, it is unlikely that you will be giving orders to your superiors. Whether you attach meaning to your role based on your profession (e.g., "I am an engineer.") or on your personal qualities (e.g., "I'm trustworthy."), the significant fact is that roles are "consciously or unconsciously assumed, assigned, accepted or declined in all human relationships" [288]. If the accepted roles are a primary constraint on the transaction, then there is a formal relationship between the two people [183]. But when knowledge of the other person is the primary constraint on the transaction, the relationship is personal. Whatever the degree of formalness, the roles that individuals assume for themselves impact on the relationship.

Two people in a transaction do not just present their desired roles to each other and then stop transacting. The roles you each assume give cues to the other about how your messages should be interpreted. These cues operate back and forth at the same time during the transaction. At a minimum, both of you (1) assume a role for yourself, (2) impute a role to the other, and (3) estimate what role the other thinks you are assuming. In Laing's terms, each dyadic participant has a direct perspective, metaperspective, and meta-metaperspective of his role and the other's role. In order for the participants to achieve any rudimentary accommodation in a relationship, each one's assumed role has to roughly correspond to the role imputed to him by the other [185]. The two individuals have to carry out reciprocally accurate acts of role attribution [156].

We as individuals define perspectives, metaperspectives, and meta-metaperspectives on our own and the other's role for one main reason. We want to have successful transactions with others. We want a place in their world, and they in ours [156]. Therefore, in our social relationships we seek support for our role-identities [186]. The sometimes awkward process of two individuals adjusting to each other is the process of *negotiation of social identities*. We define ourselves based on the other's reaction to our projected identity; we negotiate our identity with him and he negotiates his with us.

When an individual presents his assumed role—his social identity—our response to him can be characterized in one of three modes: (1) confirmation, (2) rejection, or (3) disconfirmation [330] We confirm the other's role identity when we transact in such a way as to accept him. If the chairman of a school department assigns himself to the role of parent, he wants others to need him. As a result, in his transaction he tries to be a father figure. If the other participant wants to be "fathered" or "counseled," then the relationship will probably proceed smoothly. His assumed role has been confirmed. But let's say the second participant is a faculty member who does not want a surrogate father. Then when he transacts, he will probably not confirm the chairman's desired role of parent. When this occurs, he is rejecting the role identity of the other. The negotiation of social identities is prominent; the two individuals are struggling to achieve some correspondence in their role perspectives.

The rejection of an assumed role identity can cause some disruption of the relationship if the subsequent "negotiations" do not bring the perspectives into some correspondence. In fact, the relationship may be terminated. As disruptive as this is, however, disconfirmation is potentially more damaging to the participant. In confirming or rejecting someone's assumed identity, you are agreeing or disagreeing with that person's definition of himself. But when you disconfirm the other you are *negating him* as a source of definition. You are not validating his existence! To act as if the other person does not exist has powerful effects on him. Undergraduate students in the author's classes are frequently assigned an exercise that is designed to heighten their awareness of how much we depend on others for our sense of well-being. When discussing the need for feedback, they are instructed to follow the exercise listed in Wenburg and Wilmot [334]. Namely, when they are with someone with whom they have a satisfying dyadic relationship, they try not to respond. When the other talks, they just sit still and stare through him. When the other says, "What is wrong?", no response is forthcoming. Within a few short seconds, the other person feels disconfirmation screaming at him. And it has the expected results—he typically becomes very upset. Disconfirmation by another is a frightening experience.

ISSUES AND RELATIONSHIPS

Whenever two participants communicate, the messages occur on two levels: content and relationship. For example, when the parent tells the child, "Go to bed," two messages are sent. The content message revolves around being in bed; the relationship message is that the parent has the right or obligation to tell the child what to do. In relationships where the participants treat each other as equals, their messages reinforce on the relational level how they perceive each other.

Whenever one person communicates with another, he is *defining the relationship* [113]. *It is impossible to relate to another individual only on a content basis*—relationship and content are inextricably bound together. Each individual has his own definition of the relationship and projects it when he communicates to another. The definition he has is rarely called to his or the others' attention, but it is there nevertheless. For instance, when a professor assists a student in finding materials for a project, he doesn't preface each remark with, "I have the right to help you, so read this book that I recommend." And the student doesn't say, "I'm placing myself in the position of needing help in order to borrow some of your books." Relational definitions can be indicated by who talks first, who talks the most, paralinguistic cues (tone of voice, volume, and other vocal qualities you use to say something), the seating arrangement, eye contact, and a host of other factors. Different means are used in different situations, but in all cases each participant defines the relationship.*

Not only does each participant have a direct perspective on the relationship, he has a metaperspective. He has a view of how the other person is defining their relationship. In essence, he is taking the role of the other. He modifies his "intended behavior in light of his anticipation of the other's reaction to this behavior" [86]. Each person, therefore, (1) takes the role of himself and (2) takes the role of the other. There is some dispute over whether these direct perspectives and metaperspectives are taken simultaneously or alternately, but the central issue is that one has to assume both points of view [9]. In a dyadic transaction, therefore, there is mutual adjustment to the other [266].

A specific case will illustrate part of the relationship complexity of a transaction. Person *A* and person *B* are engaged and about to be married. Person *A* wants to dominate person *B*, and *B* wants to dominate *A*. As their transaction unfolds over the issue of family finances, it is clear that each has a perspective and metaperspective on (1) the issue and (2) the relationship. On the issue of finances, *A*

---

*Furthermore, when you say, "This is how I see myself," you are really adding "in relation to you" [321].

wants two checking accounts, one in each person's name. *B* wants one account, a joint one that both will use. *A* and *B* articulate their views well and understand each other's position. On the issue there is *disagreement* (direct perspectives differ between *A* and *B*), but there is *understanding* (*A*'s metaperspective matches *B*'s direct perspective; *B*'s metaperspective matches *A*'s direct perspective). On the relationship level, the degrees of agreement/disagreement and understanding/misunderstanding become crucial to the direction the relationship takes. As the argument continues, let's assume that *A* and *B* have the perspectives and metaperspectives shown in Fig. 4-8.

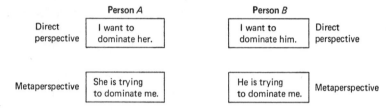

Fig. 4-8 Perspectives on a relationship.

A and *B* understand each other because both *A*'s and *B*'s metaperspectives are correct. But in this case, there is a disagreement over the relationship. *A*'s and *B*'s desires for influence in the relationship clash directly. During the continuing discussion, *A* and *B* will undoubtedly jockey for relational position. As they vie back and forth concerning the relationship, they will probably be centering their arguments around the issue of checking accounts. As the arguments over the issue come to a standstill, it is likely that someone will open up the relational issue by saying something like, "Well, I don't care about the advantages of that kind of an account—I'm the boss around here and I say we'll have the other kind!" Now the relational conflict is out in the open and the basis of the discussion has shifted from the issue to the relationship.

In any given transaction, both participants attempt to take account of themselves and the other. The direct perspective and metaperspective center around (1) the issue and (2) the relationship. There are almost infinite possibilities of degrees of agreement and degrees of understanding within a given dyad. For our purposes, however, let's consider only the most basic cases, agreement or disagreement and understanding or misunderstanding. Figure 4-9 illustrates the *least* number of possible combinations of agreement/disagreement and understanding/misunderstanding that can occur in a dyadic relationship.

(a) Issue

	Understand	Misunderstand
Agreement	(1) A/U	(2) A/M
Disagreement	(3) D/U	(4) D/M

(b) Relationship

	Understand	Misunderstand
Agreement	(5) A/U	(6) A/M
Disagreement	(7) D/U	(8) D/M

Fig. 4-9   Matching of *A*'s and *B*'s perspectives and metaperspectives on (a) an issue and (b) their relationship.*

In the illustration of persons *A* and *B* discussed above, the argument over the checking account could be characterized as occurring in cells 3 and 7 of Fig. 4-9. *A* and *B* disagreed with each other concerning the checking account and both understood the dis-

---

*This figure is a considerably shortened version of what could be constructed. It does not incorporate the metaperspectives of *A* and *B*, therefore leaving out (1) the feeling of being understood or misunderstood and (2) realization or failure of realization. Furthermore, it only shows understanding/misunderstanding when it is the same for both *A* and *B*. Obviously the case could be that *A* understands *B* and *B* misunderstands *A* or *A* misunderstands *B* and *B* understands *A*. Additionally, degrees of understanding/misunderstanding, agreement/disagreement, and the other relational characteristics could be assessed.

agreement. On the relational level, they had a similar situation—they disagreed and both understood the disagreement. The agreement/disagreement and understanding/misunderstanding on (1) the issue at hand and (2) the participants' relationship could be sketched for any continuing dyadic transaction. For instance, if a pair of individuals are engaged in a conflict, it could be due to any of the following combinations (numbers are from cells in Fig. 4–9):

(1) They agree and mutually understand each other on the issue but still have a relationship conflict (occurring in cells 6, 7, or 8).

(2) They agree on the issue but one or both participants misunderstand the other's position.

(3) They disagree on the issue and understand that they do.

(4) They disagree on the issue and, on top of that, one or both misunderstands the other's position.

(5) They agree and mutually understand each other on the relationship definition, but still have an issue conflict (occurring in cells 2, 3, or 4).

(6) They are in relational agreement but misunderstand that they are. For instance, they may misperceive each other's relational stance.

(7) They disagree relationally (both wish to control the relationship) and understand that they do.

(8) They disagree relationally and, in addition, misperceive the other's relational stance.

While this list does not represent all possible configurations that would produce conflict in a dyad, they are easily constructed. In order to represent any ongoing transaction, a cell related to both issue and relationship should be chosen. For instance, cell (1) on the issue grid would be combined with a cell from the relationship grid (cells 5–8). Similarly, issue cells 2, 3, and 4 could be combined in all possible ways with relational cells 5, 6, 7, and 8.

This analysis demonstrates that dyadic transactions can be analyzed on both issue and relational lines. For many transactions, the distinctions between the two levels become obscure. For instance, if the partners in a romantic dyad are arguing over which movie to see and the issue is not readily resolved, it will soon escalate into a full-scale relational conflict. The issue of which movie to see becomes secondary and the paramount issue is relational—who has the right to make the decision. The basis for the disagreement has shifted. In addition, it is often the case that (1) a relationship disagreement or misunderstanding will emerge as a conflict over an issue, and (2) an issue disagreement or misunderstanding may emerge as a relational conflict. Of these two cases, by far the most common is a relational disagreement acted out in terms of a particular issue. Pete had an experience along these lines. When he was growing up as a boy in a small town, a friend of his family (We'll call him Charley) exposed Pete to the fundamentals of training work horses. Charley would occasionally give assistance to ranchers and farmers who needed to train their horses for work. After Pete left home and moved to western Montana, he developed an interest in quarter horses. Having raised them for a number of years, he became proficient at the entire enterprise from selecting good horses to exhibiting them in local contests. In fact, his horses did quite well in local competitions. When he saw Charley again, they began discussing the techniques of training horses. Charley, who had only worked with rather rough work horses began arguing with Pete about the correct way to train quarter horses. The disagreement over the issue (training horses) was shifting to the relational level, each person trying to be in the role of instructing the other. From Pete's perspective, Charley was saying, "Only I can offer insight into training horses," and Pete found the relationship hard to accept.*

Such relational conflicts frequently occur in dyads. It is not uncommon, for instance, that relational conflicts between parents and teenagers are acted out in terms of a particular issue such as what time the teenager should come home. Similarly, the young child who is totally dominated by his parents may stage a fight over an issue

---

*It would be interesting to see Charley's perception of the event. One could predict that he would make relational statements such as, "Darn kids, give them a quarter horse and they think they know everything." In other words, Pete wouldn't let Charley be the only one with expertise on training.

that, to the parents, seems silly. He may, for instance, refuse to dress himself or put his toys away. Such ploys are attempts to exercise relational control by utilizing issue control.*

In the converse situation, an issue disagreement can, if not settled, erupt into a relational disagreement. If the participants are relationally in agreement but cannot solve an important issue conflict such as belief in God, relational statements are forthcoming. The author vividly recalls once having a rather heated religious disagreement. The other person, frustrated because of the lack of agreement on the issue, said, "Well, if that is what you believe, I feel sorry for you!" This relational statement, putting himself in the role of judging me, frustrated me so that the only retort I could muster was, "Well, I feel sorry for you, so we're even!"

Even though the relationship aspect is always present in dyadic communicative exchanges, individuals sometimes *try* not to define a relationship. This is done in one of four ways: (1) He may deny he sent a message by labeling himself as someone else, say a messenger of God, (2) he may deny he said something by manifesting amnesia or by claiming the other person continually misunderstands him, (3) he may deny that he is talking to the person by labeling the person as someone else, or (4) he may deny that he is in this situation by pretending he is somewhere else [112]. These four techniques are elaborate devices used to demonstrate that, from the one person's perception, he is not defining the relationship. Interestingly enough, whenever a person tries to deny defining a relationship, he is at a different level defining the relationship as one he won't define.

We maintain our transactions with others so long as the issue and relational disagreements and misunderstandings do not force termination of the relationship. The relationship hangs on more of a slender thread—mutual definition by participants—than is usually observed. Any relational threat—the spouse who cheats, the employees who derogate their employer, the Army private who refuses to salute—quickly attunes us to the fragile nature of relation-

---

*The precise linkage or overlap between the issue and relationship dimensions is an area in need of detailed research. It might be that all issue disagreements, if not resolved, have an impact on the relationship level. Furthermore, in most dyads individuals probably begin at the issue dimension and never fully discuss the relational aspects.

ships [71]. A successful transaction depends on the coordination of meaning for the participants and, at the very least, some overlap of perspectives and metaperspectives. We usually agree and understand the other well enough "to work out a sort of fumbling, on-again, off-again accommodation in which we manage to get along with, and past, one another without serious conflict" [185]. Hopefully, this excursion into the content and relationship aspects of dyadic communicative exchanges has highlighted the fact that consideration of both issue and relationship perspectives is important.

DIMENSIONS OF RELATIONSHIPS

Knowing that dyadic participants communicate on a relationship as well as an issue basis is important information. But in addition, one should also be aware of the bases for the relationship perspectives that develop. The function of this next section is to explain those bases.

The bases of relationships have been viewed from many vantage points. Kurth's [153] system assesses the voluntariness, uniqueness, intimacy, and obligations of participants. Alternative schemes of analysis have been formulated by Yablonsky [349], McCall [183], Ruesch [244], Jackson [135], and popular writers such as Goffman [103]. However, a detailed review of each of these notions of relationship would be more confusing than enlightening. A summary by Carson [51a] demonstrates that there is a vast amount of empirical literature that can be summarized in a meaningful manner. The research that Carson reviews demonstrates quite dramatically that:

> On the whole, the conclusion seems justified that major portions of the domain of interpersonal behavior can profitably and reasonably accurately be conceived as involving variations on two independent bipolar dimensions. One of these may be called a *dominance/submission* dimension; it includes dominant, assertive, ascendant, leading, controlling (etc.) behavior on one hand, and submissive, retiring, obsequious, unassertive, following (etc.) behavior on the other. The poles of the second principal dimension are perhaps best approximated by the terms *hate* versus *love*; the former includes hateful, aggressive, rejecting, punishing, attacking, disaffiliative (etc.) behavior, while the lat-

ter includes accepting, loving, affectionate, affiliative, friendly (etc.) social actions [51a].*

Any dyadic relationship can be characterized as having two components: (1) dominance/submission and (2) love/hate. In other words, in terms of the relational component of any dyadic transaction, the participants relate to each other by expressing behavior centered around control of each other (or lack of it) and affection (positive and negative).

Timothy Leary's [162] work on the dimensions of relationships probably best illustrates how one can use these two dimensions of relationships to characterize communication styles. A person who is competitive, for instance, is manifesting both a desire to control the other person (dominance) and some hostility (hate). A person's cooperative behavior is best characterized as somewhere between dominance and submission, while at the same time demonstrating positive affection (love). Figure 4–10 is a reproduction of Leary's behavioral classifications.

Leary specifies that interpersonal reflexes are prominent in our transactions with others. A reflex is a probable response that one almost "automatically" makes. For instance, when someone says to you, "I hate you," your reflex action is probably one of like nature (a dislike for the other person). Dominating or bossing someone provokes its opposite, obedience. Leary's circumplex, the circular arrangement of behaviors around the dimensions of dominance/submission and love/hate, can be summarized as follows:

1. Behavior on the love/hate dimension provokes similar behavior. Love provokes love; hostility provokes hostility.

---

*The research supporting this conclusion is fascinating, but because of the amount of detail involved to present it, it is omitted here. Carson's book is superb and should be read by anyone wishing more detail on the dimensions of dyadic behavior.

One noted theorist, William C. Schutz [267], postulates that there are three interpersonal needs—control, inclusion, and affection. Carson suggests that Schutz's control dimension is similar to the dominance/submission dimension, and that love/hate is an amalgamation of Schutz's inclusion and affection dimensions [51a].

2. Behavior on the dominance/submission dimension provokes its complement. Being submissive provokes leadership behavior in the other; managing and directing provoke obedience.

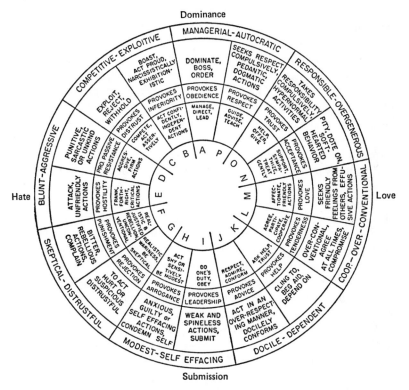

Each of the 16 interpersonal variables is illustrated by sample behaviors. The inner circle names adaptive reflexes, such as *manage*. Proceeding outward, the next ring indicates the type of behavior that this interpersonal reflex tends to 'pull' from the other one; thus the person who uses the reflex A tends to call up in others *obedience*. These findings involve two-way interpersonal phenomena—what the subject does and what the other does in return—and are therefore less reliable than the other interpersonal categories presented in the inner and outer rings. The next circle illustrates extreme or rigid reflexes, such as *dominates*. The perimeter of the circle is divided into eight general categories employed in interpersonal diagnosis. Each of these general categories has a moderate (adaptive) and an extreme (pathological) intensity, such as *managerial-autocratic*.

Fig. 4-10 Leary's circumplex—classification of interpersonal behavior into 16 mechanisms or reflexes. (From Timothy Leary, "The Theory and Measurement Methodology of Interpersonal Communication," *Psychiatry* **18** (May 1955):147–161. By permission.)

In order to fully discuss the implications the two dimensions have for dyadic relationships, they will be treated separately. Note, however, that the two dimensions are woven together in dyadic transactions. If you as a participant perceive the other's behavior as hostile, it will likely trigger hostile behavior in you. And the same perceptual-based behavior would be applicable to the other participant.

Dominance/Submission.   If two communication participants agree on the control aspects of their relationship, struggles over dominance/submission are likely to be minimal. For example, in a friendship dyad, if each participant expects to exercise some dominant and some submissive behavior, and each does, there will be no difficulties encountered on the dominance/submission dimension. On the other hand, if both participants wish to control the relationship, definite struggles over dominance will occur. For instance, in a romantic dyad, if both individuals try to dominate the other, a "lover's quarrel" will ensue. The difficulty comes about because there is a tendency for different roles to develop; the individuals are expected to accommodate each other. In Leary's terms, if an instructor is trying to direct a student to read a good book on communication, the student is expected to jot down the title and heed the advice, namely, to give the proper reflex behavior. However, if every time a book title is suggested he suggests one for the instructor to read, the instructor's expectation has been violated. Most of us expect the other to respond to our attempts at authority by accepting such attempts (by being submissive).

   The dominance/submission aspect of relationships can be best characterized by labeling relationships as *complementary*, *symmetrical*, or *parallel*. In a complementary relationship, each person's behavior complements the other's. The relationship is based on differences; one person primarily is dominant. A mother and young child are in a complementary relationship—the mother is superior, the child inferior (until the baby cries in the middle of the night). A boss-employee relationship is complementary, as are those between teacher-student, doctor-patient, policeman-automobile driver, president-secretary, and other relationships based on inequality of control. "One partner occupies what has been variously described as the superior, primary, or 'one-up' position and the other the corresponding inferior, secondary, or 'one-down' position" [330]. One person initiates action and the other follows it [135]. In such a relationship, both individuals need each other because the "dissimilar but fitted behaviors evoke each other" [330]. A woman needs a child in order to be a mother; a boss without any employees is no boss; a doctor cannot doctor anyone unless he has a patient. Likewise, the person in the less dominant position needs the other person. Both participants are fulfilled by the actions of the other [156].

There is nothing necessarily dysfunctional or harmful about relationships based on complementary needs for dominance. In fact, complementary relationships enable us as dyadic participants to share in the expertise of the other. While you are in the submissive position, you can absorb from others what they have to offer. A student, for instance, can gain insight by letting a professor be dominant over the relationship; he can "pick the professor's brain." And it is probably wise for the professor to engage in transactions with a student where the student is the dominant one. It could be argued that people who are accustomed to dominant role positions can learn the most by engaging in communication interchanges where the two participants engage in periodic role reversals. The doctor should be a patient, the teacher a student, and the social worker a client. Similarly, it probably would be wise to assign the dominant position to individuals who usually cannot define the relationship. When, for example, student-teacher roles are reversed, the student will likely discover the role of teacher may not be as dominant as he first thought. Role reversals in dyads can illuminate the dominant dimension of the relationship and, if someone refuses to reverse roles, he is simply affirming that he likes the way his role is presently defined.

By the way we communicate, we are always defining the dominant/submissive dimension of our relationships. If the other person attempts to exercise dominance over you, you do not have to accept his definition. You always have the option of refusing the other's definition of the relationship and supplying your own [282]. But any definition you advance has its consequences. If you give the expected reflex behavior by being submissive, the transaction may proceed smoothly, but you could be frustrated by the lack of control. If you attempt to redefine the relationship by exercising dominance over the other, a struggle over the relationship will likely develop. If the two of you establish equality over dominance, a *symmetric* relationship has developed [330].

In symmetric relationships, the participants behave as if they have equal status. Close friendships, for instance, are often dyads based on equality. Both individuals are free to exercise control; they both have the same options available. "Each person exhibits the right to initiate action, criticize the other, offer advice and so on" [135].

At first glance, symmetric relationships may appear to be the most desirable ones. After all, if the participants treat each other as equals, then struggles over dominance should disappear. Usually, however, the dominance issue is more unsettled than in a complementary relationship. When people treat each other as equals, they are not ignoring dominance, they are in competition for it [135]. Whereas in a complementary relationship the rights of dominance are clearly defined, in symmetric relationships rights of dominance are constantly being redefined. For instance, ". . . if one person mentions that he has succeeded in some endeavor the other person mentions that he has succeeded in an equally important endeavor" [135].

The dominance/submission dimension is always present in dyadic relationships.* One cannot *not* define the relationship. Put another way, each individual will act upon his direct perspective, metaperspective, and meta-metaperspective concerning control of the relationship. Furthermore, the definition of the relationship by the participants will often change. When conversation shifts from topic to topic, so may the dominance. In fact, in informal dyadic transactions, each person has areas he defines. When this is the case, as it often is, the relationship is *parallel* [135]. In parallel relationships there are frequent "crossovers" between complementary and symmetric relationships [135]. There is some evidence to indicate that if a relationship is parallel, namely, that if both complementary and symmetric definitions occur, the transactions are less rigid and less inclined to be pathological [165, 197, 282, 330]. The implications of parallel transactions and of transactions that are exclusively symmetric or complementary are just being explored [216]. Without doubt however, the control dimension of dyadic relationships is a crucial aspect of any transaction.

---

*It is also obviously present in all interpersonal relationships. In a public speaking situation, for instance, the system norms define who is to be dominant, the speaker. The more informal or personal the communication transaction, the freer the participants are to define dominance.

Love/Hate. The other major dimension that emerges in communicative exchanges is affection and hostility, or love/hate. As noted in the opening chapter, it is in dyads that the best and worst emotions come to the surface. Romantic dyads, as a case in point, range from pairs in which each would give their life in order to save their partner's to those in which one takes the life of the partner—clear expressions of love and hate. Most dyadic transactions, however, have degrees of hostility or affection that are between the two extremes, but they can be characterized as possessing predominately affection or hostility.

Dyadic transactions that are characterized by hostility can take many forms. In the more extreme case, an anti-pair can be formed. In such a dyad, the participants heap abuse and malice on each other and the dyad functions because petty nagging and scolding, threats and counterthreats become behaviors that the partners cannot do without [320]. The dyad is woven together by the hostility rather than dissolved by it. Sometimes participants express hostility because they have not learned how to express the positive feelings they possess. The person who is always compelled to make snide remarks, who continuously plays one-upmanship, or who is always trying to impress others with his intellect is doing one thing—he is rejecting others so they will accept him. If he truly loves someone, yet constantly "puts the other down" in public, he is simply disguising positive affection in the clothing of hostility. The person receiving the put-downs, however, may find it increasingly hard to always interpret the negative remarks as positive.

The hostility felt between two individuals is often not openly expressed. When the secretary really hates the boss, or the student dislikes the teacher, the feelings are often not shared. Instead of openly expressing the hostility, it is covered up and related to someone else. The students swapping tales of "Isn't that teacher terrible," the wives having coffee and complaining about their husbands, or the husbands discussing how they dislike their wives are all attempts to deal with hostility. It is gossip which is "an unhealthy way of creating one relationship by betraying another" [13].

Transactions also express varying degrees of positive emotion. Close dyads thrive on affection. To show positive regard for someone is to accept him, thereby increasing the chances of him accepting you. Put another way, as a dyadic relationship becomes more positive, the participants will tend to disclose more positive emotions. Until certain upper limits are reached, positive affect provokes positive affect [64, 81, 346].

The differences between types of dyads can at least be partially explained by the expected level of expressing positive feelings. It might be somewhat awkward if employees continually tell their employer, "I love you." By the same token, if a marital dyad has no more intimacy and positive affection than a friendship dyad has, it may be a "surface marriage." It shows all the outward signs of a strongly committed marital dyad, but the crucial element of a strong bond of affection is missing. On the other hand, expecting too much positive affection, similar relational difficulties can arise. As anyone who has tried to snuggle up to a romantic partner who wants only friendship can attest, there are differences in expected affection.

The expression of positive affection does not have to be dramatic. You do not have to run up and kiss someone in front of God and everybody in order to show positive affection. In all types of dyads, it is often sufficient to pay attention to someone, give them a smile, or just be responsive to their existence. The individual who fails to become fully involved with another is called a "cold fish" or "wet blanket" [103], both of which say, "You are not giving me positive affection; you do not respond to my existence."

This discussion of the two dimensions of dyadic relationships has devoted a separate section to an explanation of each dimension. But in an actual transaction, of course, the two dimensions jointly characterize specific behaviors. Refer again to Fig. 4–10. By closely examining Leary's circumplex, you can see that interpersonal behaviors reflect a blend of the two dimensions. Each behavioral act reflects some degree of dominance/submission and some degree of love/hate. These two dimensions, therefore, are central to all dyadic processes.

RECIPROCITY: A DYADIC NORM

In any successful dyad, the norm of reciprocity exists. Whether a person is walking down the street and says "Hi" to you or gives you a birthday present, you feel the need to respond to the other's behavior. In dyadic relationships, reciprocity "implies that the behavior of either party is contingent to some degree on the perceived behavior of the other . . ." [255]. You expect the other person's behavior to be somewhat contingent on your own. In fact, in mutually beneficial and satisfying relationships, a reciprocal element can be found. Each person's behavior is, in some respect, mututally contingent on the other's [108]. Reciprocity does *not* mean that the behaviors of any two persons are identical. It does mean that each one's behavior is affected by the behavior of the other. The two individuals are bound together in a relationship.

Relationships develop in stages, and as they do, the demands for reciprocity are likewise altered. In initial transactions the participants orient themselves to each other, and as a relationship develops over a period of time, the participants expose more and more of themselves to each other [6]. Concomitant with these relationship changes, reciprocity demands are altered. In initial encounters, awareness of and attention to the other are reciprocal demands. As the relationship progresses, the reciprocity expectations are increased so that participants expect behaviors that will fulfill their needs. These expectations for reciprocity are apparently universal and, while they are being met, add stability to relationships [108].

Reciprocal behaviors take three main forms: (1) nonreciprocal behaviors, (2) symmetrical reciprocal behaviors, and (3) asymmetrical reciprocal behaviors [255]. One of the best examples of nonreciprocal behavior is two people speaking on the telephone, each one ignoring what the other says. Piaget, in his studies of children, labeled it "parallel play" when two children are next to each other but neither's behavior is contingent on the other's. In essence, *no relationship* has been formed because each one is implicitly saying, "I see myself," rather than saying, "I see you seeing me."* For someone who expects the other to respond to him, such nonreciprocal behaviors can be quite disruptive.

Symmetrical reciprocal behaviors are those in which the behavior of each is contingent on the behavior of the other. It can occur in friendship, romantic, and generation dyadic transactions. Using the terminology introduced earlier, a symmetrical relationship in which each party has the right to dominate would manifest such reciprocal behaviors. In addition, the affection behaviors from each

---

*Jones and Thibaut [143] label this as "noncontingent interaction." Wenburg and Wilmot [325] label it the "mother-in-law syndrome." Sarbin, Taft, and Bailey [255] present three subcategories of nonreciprocal behavior. They are not discussed here because they are inconsistent with the terminology and analysis presented earlier in this chapter.

would be closely related. Each person takes his cue from the behavior of the other. Obviously if a dyadic transaction is highly structured, the behaviors are prescribed and not responsive to the other participant.

Transactions characterized by role behavior on one person's part and contingent behavior on the other's are asymmetrical reciprocal. One person initiates the bulk of the communication and the other is confined to reciprocate. Aider-aided dyads, for instance, are characterized this way. The physician has his duties to perform, but the patient must give reciprocating behaviors. The interviewer has a structured inventory of programmed behaviors, and the client has to respond to those. In asymmetrical reciprocal transactions, one person has a role obligation to perform or is more powerful than the other. In either case the patient, client, or subordinate is expected to do all the adjusting. The transaction is clearly complementary on both dominance/submission and love/hate dimensions. One individual sets both dimensions in motion because of his role, and the other must reciprocate.

The one-sidedness of reciprocity in asymmetrically contingent transactions is not necessarily disruptive to a particular dyad [108]. Many dyads that are long-lasting thrive on their complementariness or asymmetry. But (when both expect the other to reciprocate), if one member continually receives more benefits than the other, problems will develop [22]. In a romantic dyad, if the husband places himself above reciprocation and the wife wants him to reciprocate, frictions will occur. Serving your needs at the expense of the other works only as long as the other lets you.

Dyadic relationships continue only when reciprocity is present to some degree. If the behaviors of neither partner are not contingent on the other's behavior, then no relationship can be formed or maintained. The participants are simply engaged in behaviors isolated from each other. It is sufficient if one person is held primarily responsible for reciprocation, for if he is, the two participants are still able to say, "I see you seeing me." For instance, during a highly structured interview in which all of the interviewer's questions are preplanned, he will not move to the next question until the interviewee has given a reciprocal behavior. While one person is more constrained by his role, both parties take cues from the other and then select their next behavior. Their behaviors are reciprocal and mutual adjustment is occurring.

SUMMARY

The proper focus for the study of dyadic communication is at the relationship level. A relationship is formed when participants are mutually aware of each other, and the comparison of their various perspectives yields insights into the relationship *per se*. Through their perceptions, participants negotiate their views of themselves and the other and relate to each other on (1) issues and (2) the relationship between them. The relationship between the participants occurs on two basic dimensions, love/hate and dominance/submission. Furthermore, in dyadic relationships, there exists a norm of reciprocity; each one's behavior is contingent upon the other's. Clearly, dyadic communication is relational in nature.

Chapter 5

Relational Intricacies: Self-fulfilling Prophecies, Spirals, Paradoxes, and Do-Loops

Whereas the previous chapter outlined the bases for a relationship approach to the study of dyads, this chapter focuses on relational intricacies. The complexity that characterizes dyadic relationships can be best understood by examining some of the intricate turns that relationships can take.

SELF-FULFILLING PROPHECIES

> If men define situations as real, they are real
> in their consequences.
>
> —W. I. Thomas

> A tremendous number of things we believe in,
> because we see them done, are done for no other
> reason except that we believe in them.
>
> —Wendell Johnson

Each of us defines our own world and acts on the basis of those definitions. The perspectives we have of ourselves and others determine our actions and, in turn, our actions determine our perspectives. "Man lives by propositions whose validity is a function of his belief in them" [248]. When we are in a communicative relationship with another person, the definitions of each and the correspondence between them determine the character of the relationship.

A self-fulfilling prophecy is one of the more dramatic examples of the impact one's definition of a situation can have on behavior. It is a *"false* definition of the situation, evoking a new behavior which makes the originally false conception come true" [196]. The prophecy leads to its own fulfillment! For instance, if a bank is financially sound, but a rumor of its insolvency becomes believed by enough depositors, the subsequent run on the bank will result in insolvency. The human definition of a situation becomes an integral part of the situation, and therefore affects the situation.

Merton's analysis of self-fulfilling prophecies is a valuable contribution to social theory. In terms of human communication, however, the initial definition of a situation *may or may not be false.* One can observe a bank before the run on it and determine if it is solvent or not. But how can you look at another individual and determine if he is one who can be trusted, for example? Such assessments of another can rarely be made, if ever, with any certainty. But if you think the person cannot be trusted and you act distrustful of him, he will likely respond appropriately. Your definition of the other will often create the behavior you thought was there. Whether he was initially untrustworthy is a moot issue. You cannot know if your original definition was true or false, because whatever your definition initially was, it is always part of the situation.

Self-fulfilling prophecies occur because an original definition of a situation by one participant is acted upon by a second participant responding appropriately. Sequentially, the process goes like this:

1. Person A makes an inference about person B.
2. A acts toward B in terms of this inference.
3. B makes inferences about A in terms of this action.
4. B tends to react toward A in terms of this inference.
5. Thus A's inferences tend to be confirmed by B's actions [185].

The paradoxical aspect of self-fulfilling prophecies is that when we are caught in one, we do not know it. We act on the basis of our definition because we treat it as an accurate understanding of the situation. When our definition is acted upon, it is necessarily part of the situation.* Once the system begins operating, however, each individual typically does not see his own behavior as part of the system, though it necessarily is. "A and B claim to be reacting to the partner's behavior without realizing that they in turn influence the partner by their reaction" [330]. In a triadic situation, when two people form a coalition and reject person C, C's response to the rejection typically validates the coalition's actions. After all, A and B had to form a pair because C was hostile to them. The effect of the action became a justification for it.

Instances of self-fulfilling prophecies are numerous. A mother's anxiety about a child affects her behavior such that the child, re-

---

*It is obvious that not all dyadic transactions illustrate self-fulfilling prophecies. For instance, when B does not interpret A's behavior as A intended, or when B counters with a different definition, A's original definition cannot go the full circle of creating what he thought he saw. Also, when there are institutional controls that constrain participants from responding fully to each other, self-fulfilling prophecies cannot operate [196].

sponding to her anxious state, becomes difficult and worrisome to care for. The child's behavior becomes the cause as well as effect of the mother's anxiety [296]. Once an individual is classified as mentally ill, others will often respond to that definition be reinforcing "sick" behavior [99]. Let's assume for a moment that you are sitting home watching television when there is a knock at the door. Three large men in white uniforms burst into the room shouting, "There he is, get him!" As they wrestle you to the floor, you scream violent protest (in between biting and kicking). At the point where they have you under control, they show you a court order committing you to a mental institution because of your aggressive and violent behavior against your relatives, though you know your relatives are committing you unjustly. Once in the institution you are released from the restraint. You demand to see the director, pleading that it is all some horrible mistake. When he comes to your ward, you explain the circumstances. He says, "There now, it's all right. A lot of us think we are something we are not." The more you protest, the less convinced he becomes, so you protest more vigorously. As you shake him and scream, "I am not violent," the attendants slap a straightjacket on you. The prophecy is fulfilled.*

Examples of self-fulfilling prophecies are not only numerous, but they arise in diverse situations. It has been noted for many years that the way you classify a person can determine your general reaction to him. In the case of stuttering, "The parents classified their children as stutterers and then proceeded to react to them largely in terms of the implications of the label" [141]. Similarly, if one classifies a black person as being a meagre performer, the black in a job interview will be treated to nonverbal cues so he perceives the interviewer as cold. Then as a result, he performs less adequately [345].

Prophecies can also be initiated based on how we define ourselves. Persons who view themselves as socially adept are the ones who act toward others with skill and elicit positive responses. The

---

*A television episode of "Owen Marshall, Counselor at Law" carried a story similar to this. The patient, once committed, is reinforced for the very behaviors that he was incarcerated for. One of the few effective ways to escape is to (1) admit that you are ill and need help, and (2) slowly improve your behavior so the staff members think they are "curing" you. Protesting too much simply validates their prophecy.

positive response from another cycles back and convinces a person that he is socially adept. Similarly, if one has a low opinion of how he relates to others, this may produce behaviors such as nervousness, small amounts of eye contact, and an inability to form an effective bond with the other. The other, reacting to your projected inability to relate to him, gives you negative responses—which confirm your initial definition [59].

A communication researcher's viewpoint of communication can become a prophecy which validates itself. If you as a researcher believe in the assumptions of the scientific method, then the data will likely reinforce that view. If communication is to you a set of cause-and-effect, linear relationships, you carry this definition with you. When you design an experiment, you do it to ferret out relationships. So, what do the data tell you? That there are cause-and-effect relationships between the variables. By forcing such a linear view on the process, you "become blind to the cybernetic circularities" that are present [20]. Communication researchers, as well as those in other fields, operate similarly to the layman. In order to understand a process, we have to stop it, punctuate the events, and apply causal analysis. While such punctuation is necessary, one can never be sure that his ordering of events has accurately identified the events [51a]. And if this notion has merit, that our definition defines what we see, then the transactional approach taken in this book is just as circular and self-fulfilling as the traditional linear approach. The test of "truth," therefore, can never be made. *One can only examine a particular approach in terms of the utility it has.* Just as in dyadic self-fulfilling prophecies, the truth or falsity of the original definition can probably not be established.

Self-fulfilling prophecies operate full-blown in our educational institutions. Rosenthal's work has shown that the expectation a teacher has of a student can lead to its own fulfillment. One of the latest reported studies is typical [239a]. The researchers selected an elementary school in a lower-class neighborhood and administered an IQ test to all the children. The test was disguised as one that would predict "intellectual blooming." Twenty percent of the children in each room were randomly selected as "bloomers," and the teachers were told that these children would make remarkable gains in test scores during the next year. The only differences between the children were in the teachers' minds. Eight months later, when the children were retested, the children that teachers had been led to believe were going to bloom did. They showed an average additional gain of four IQ points over the children who teachers did not expect to bloom [239, 239a]. The teachers' expectations benefited students. While there have been some objections to Rosenthal's work, the data at this point lend fairly strong credence to the notion that self-fulfilling prophecies exist in classrooms.*

Of course, the prophecy need not be a positive one. Garfield, Weiss, and Pollack [98] used a procedure similar to Rosenthal's, only this time with school counselors. The counselors were divided into two groups and given identical descriptions of a boy with behavior problems typical of the type the counselors often handled. One group was given information that the boy came from the upper-middle social class, and the other group was given information clearly indicating that the boy was from a lower-class background. The social class descriptions had a significant impact on the counselors' projected reactions. The counselors were more willing "to become ego-involved in the management of the child who is seen as 'more important' and worthier of attention" than the youngster who comes from the lower class. "By passively accepting the expectancy of unfavorable outcome, the counselor all too frequently contributes to the 'inevitability' of events" [98].

Knowing how self-fulfilling prophecies operate, we can put them to work for us. The example cited in the second chapter about the girl graduate student who had her self-concept raised is an excellent case in point. The suitors, other graduate students, redefined her as a desirable girl, and she became one. If the participant responds to your definition of him, you can remake him to be what you describe him to be [73]. We all know the classic old-timer who assumes others love him and, "by acting on his assumption, actually gets them to do so" [73].

"What you see is what you get." Even though a cliche, knowledge of this principle has assisted junior high students in a Visalia, California school in becoming more effective students and happier with school. The students who were incorrigible were typically re-

---

*Rosenthal calls it the "pygmalion effect," based on Ovid and George Bernard Shaw's play of how Henry Higgins transformed Eliza Doolittle from an illiterate peasant girl to a proper lady based on his expectations of her.

moved from regular classes and placed in classes for students with behavioral problems. Unknown to the regular classroom teachers, the "problem" students were given training in behavioral modification. Upon returning to the classroom, the students began looking for positive responses from the teachers. When the teachers gave positive responses, they (the teachers) were rewarded. While the students had some difficulty in praising teachers sincerely, they soon became skillful. The smiling, attentive students had teachers actually liking them after a few weeks [109]. The effects of the dyadic behaviors came full circle and the "delinquents" performed better in school and liked it more. These effects came about because of the teachers' responses to the students. In this case, the cyclical positive responses were the result of teachers who:

- created a warmer social-emotional mood around their "special" students;
- gave more feedback to these students about their performance;
- taught more material and more difficult material to their special students;
- gave their special students more opportunities to respond and question [239a].

Self-fulfilling prophecies can be utilized to our and others' advantages. If you search for and reward constructive elements in dyadic relationships, those relationships can become more and more positive. What you look for is what you see, and what you see is what you get.

SPIRALS

Once a dyadic transaction has come into existence, the circularity of dyadic communication becomes apparent. Each action is input into an ongoing, cyclic system. The circular effects of participant responses are the stepping stones to the existence of self-fulfilling prophecies. Each person refracts the expectations of the other in what becomes an endless circularity. One's original definition of a situation becomes validated in the transaction.

Self-fulfilling prophecies, as interesting as they may be, do not fully describe the dynamism of transactions. In most communicative interchanges, both people add energy to the system. If the definitions of the two add to each other, a spiral relationship occurs. In a self-fulfilling prophecy, A's original definition is validated. In a relationship spiral, A's definition is *intensified* by B's reaction.

Two nondyadic illustrations should clarify the essential nature of spirals. The author's three-year-old son Jason saw a sleek, shiny cat one day. With the reckless abandonment of a child his age, he rushed at the cat to pet it. The wise cat, seeing potential death, moved out of Jason's reach. Not to be outdone ("Surely the cat can't be evading me."), Jason tried harder. The cat moved farther away. Jason started running after the cat. The cat, no dummy about life, ran too. In a short ten seconds from the initial lunge at the cat, Jason and the cat were running at full tilt.*

According to one source, the Eskimos used knowledge of spirals to kill wolves. The hunters would take a hunting knife, coat the blade with whale blubber, and ram the handle into the snow with the blubberized blade pointing skyward. When a wolf passed by the knife long after the hunters left, the smell would attract him. He would lick the blubber . . . it tasted good, so he would again. Soon the edges of the knife protruded only slightly enough to barely slice a small cut in his tongue. The blood flowing on the blubber made the wolf more excited and he would begin biting the blubber. The more he bit, the more he bled. The more blood that flowed, the more frenzied he became. He soon died in a pool of his own blood, having been caught in a vicious spiral.

Dyadic participants frequently find themselves in spirals [151]. Romantic dyads, for instance, find themselves advancing through threat and counterthreat so far that they reach a point of no return [297]. The I-wish-I-had-not-said-that feeling after an argument gives testimony to the spiraling effects that build in relationships. Such a building of responses produces a lock-step effect in relationships [162]. On the positive side, "Friendship is like a fishhook; the further it goes in, the harder it is to pull out" [297]. Communication spirals,

---

*The cat was faster and survived to run another day.

whether they head in positive or negative directions, are characterized by these elements:

1. The participants' meanings intertwine in such a way that each person's behavior accelerates the dynamism of the relationship. The relational synergy builds upon itself in a continuously accelerating manner.

2. In any given period of time, a dyadic spiral is building in either a progressive or regressive direction. Progressive spirals fulfill participants' needs and usually promote positive feelings about the relationship; regressive spirals are harmful to participants' needs and move the relationship toward dissolution.

3. Unless progressive and regressive spirals are checked by the limits of the participants' toleration, they become either dysfunctional or the dyadic relationship is dissolved.

4. Any spiral can be changed, its pace quickened or slowed or its direction reversed by the participants' actions.

Progressive Spirals.   When participants serve each other's needs such that A's acts reinforce B, and B's acts reinforce A, the synergy of the system makes the relationship progressively better. Positive or progressive spirals occur such that each participant feels more and more positive toward the other. For instance, the teacher who can be open and accepting of students can often experience such spirals. Searching for the positive in a student and rewarding it appropriately can open a student up for teacher influence. The more genuinely the teacher relates to the student, the better the student performs; the higher the quality of his performance, the more positive the teacher can become.

Positive spirals are obviously not limited to teacher-student dyads. In all dyadic transactions, as A responds to B in a manner B regards as appropriate, B's behaviors are reinforced. His sense of identity is strengthened and his ability to relate to A improves [277]. Jourard [144] titles the acceleration of the system as the "dyadic effect." Each person's actions feed more energy into a system of relations that, like fusion, continues to build. The case of the highly motivated worker illustrates the same ever-widening nature of spirals. A highly motivated person strives to improve working conditions; the improved working conditions increase the worker's motivation, which cycles back and makes for an even better climate, which increases . . . .

In progressive spirals, the perceptions of the partners become more accurate and their mutual adjustments continue to build [39, 304]. In romantic dyads, "love generates more love, growth more growth, and knowledge more knowledge" [214]. The favorableness builds upon itself. Trust and understanding cycle back to create more trust and understanding. The relationship is precisely like a spiral—ever-widening. In abstract terms, Fig. 5-1 is a diagram of the ever-increasing positive aspect of progressive spirals. As the transaction continues, the positive effects keep accelerating.

Fig. 5-1   A progressive spiral.

Progressive spirals can be identified in a number of cases that relate to communication, whether dyadic or not. We all get caught in progressive spirals. The student who begins doing work of a high caliber, earns better grades, and becomes self-motivated enters a progressive spiral. Each piece of work brings a reward (good grades or praise) that further encourages him to feats of excellence. And if conditions are favorable, the spiral can continue to progress. Or the college professor (yours truly) who writes a book can enter a progressive spiral. By making a contribution and becoming more knowledgeable, he discovers that he has more to offer students. The excited students (I hope), in turn, reinforce his desire to work hard so he can feel even better about his profession. In progressive spirals, the actions of the individual supply a multiplier effect in reinforcement. The better you do, the more worthwhile you feel; the more worthwhile you feel, the better you do. The effects of a simple action reverberate throughout the system. An unexpected tenderness, for instance, will not stop with your loved one. It will recycle back to you, and probably come from you again in increased dosage.

Regressive Spirals.   Regressive spirals are mirror images of progressive spirals; the process is identical but the results are opposite. Figure 5–1 showing a progressive spiral is also an appropriate diagram of a regressive spiral in which misunderstanding and discord create more and more relationship damage. As with progressive spirals, regressive spirals take many forms.

The inability to reach out and develop meaningful relationships can often compound itself. The person who has reduced interest in others and does not form effective relationships suffers a lower self-esteem (because self-esteem is socially derived), which in turn cycles back and produces less interest in others. "The process is cyclical and degenerative" [349a]. Or if one is afraid to love others, he shuns people, which in turn makes it more difficult to love. Also, such regressive spirals often happen to people with regard to their sense of worth concerning work. The person who has not established himself in his profession (whether he be a college professor, life insurance salesman, or anything else), and yet has been in the profession for a number of years, may get caught in a spiral. He may spend his time trying to appear busy, gossiping about others or using various techniques to establish some sense of worth. Behavior that can change the spiral—working hard or retraining—are those least likely to occur. It is a self-fulfilling prophecy with a boost—it gets worse and worse. With each new gamut or ploy perfected (acquiring a new hobby, joining numerous social gatherings, etc.), the real issues become farther submerged.

Regressive cycles are readily apparent when a relationship begins disintegrating. When distrust feeds distrust, defensiveness soars and the relationship worsens, and such "runaway relationships" become destructive for all concerned [13]. In a "gruesome twosome," for instance, the two participants maintain a close, negative relationship. Each person receives fewer gratifications from the relationship, yet they maintain the attachment by mutual exploitation [259]. Gruesome twosomes can occur in almost any dyadic pairing. When the relationship prevents one or both partners from gratifying normal needs, yet the relationship is maintained, the twosome is caught in a regressive spiral.

Hostility builds the patterns for an increase in hostility, and once an interpersonal conflict begins, "These mutual effects create the possibility of a quick spiraling of events toward dangerous levels of conflict . . ." [213]. Such a "pendulum effect" was evidenced in a study by Zimbardo [350]. Using volunteers, Zimbardo created an artifical prison and used seventy volunteers. Half of the people were arbitrarily designated as prisoners and half as guards. After only six days, the mock prison had to be closed down. The "guards" treated the "prisoners" as if they were despicable animals and the "prisoners" became servile, dehumanized robots. The volunteers had advanced so far into the regressive spirals structured by the accepted roles of guards and prisoners that the mock prison became a reality. Each day the "guards" became more brutal and the "prisoners" more de-humanized.

Regressive spirals are evident in many situations. Unless they are modified into progressive spirals, they will typically lead to the dissolution of the relationship—quitting the job, beating the prisoner, or, in the case the little prince, nowhere:

"I am drinking," replied the tippler, with a lugubrious air.

"Why are you drinking?" demanded the little prince.

"So that I may forget," replied the tippler.

"Forget what?" inquired the little prince, who already was sorry for him.

"Forget that I am ashamed," the tippler confessed, hanging his head.

"Ashamed of what?" insisted the little prince, who wanted to help him.

"Ashamed of drinking!" The tippler brought his speech to an end, and shut himself up in an impregnable silence.

And the little prince went away, puzzled [72].

Alternating Spirals. Figure 5-1, while it accurately portrays the ever-increasing nature of both progessive and regressive spirals, has one major weakness. It gives the impression that a spiral, once begun, has no limits and continues unabated. All communication spirals, however, have limited boundaries. Take the case of an individual with a high self-concept. His self-concept promotes positive responses from others, which in turn enhance his self-concept. Such a pro-gressive spiral, however, has limiting boundaries. If the person's self-concept continues to be encouraged, he will eventually reach the stage at which he considers himself superior to others. At that point, negative responses from others will go to work on him to lower his self-concept. Without such limiting actions, the person's high self-concept will soon become dysfunctional in his relationships. A progressive spiral will either whirl away unchecked and break a relationship, or short regressive phases will occasionally slow it down. In either event, it is clear that progressive spirals cannot continue unabated.

Regressive spirals also have limits. A dyadic conflict, if unchecked or without redeeming features, will lead to the dissolution of the relationship. A person with a low self-concept can suffer only so much continuing maladjustment with others. A romantic pair caught in a regressive spiral will eventually move back to less destructive behaviors or else dissolve the relationship. Even the special case of the "gruesome twosome" is similar. In this case the constant bickering and quarreling are still done within limits; it is only that on the average the transactions are tolerated on a more destructive level than is usual.

Dyadic relationships, if they are maintained, fluctuate between progessive and regressive spirals. In addition to fluctuating between progessive and regressive stages, relationships can be typified over points in time as being primarily progressive or regressive. Take the case of a marital dyad. The relationship begins as a progessive spiral. The two are in love, and the mutually rewarding behaviors of both participants keep the system healthy. But due to the husband often being away from home, regressive spirals, rather than being an occasional event, become the norm. In Fig. 5–2, the fluctuation of the relationship can be seen.

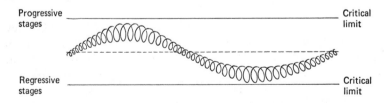

Fig. 5–2   Progressive and regressive spiral phases of a marital dyad.

The relationship continues to disintegrate into ever-regressive stages until the critical limit of the regressive spiral is reached.* As the relationship begins passing the critical limit, the patterns of regressiveness become more and more difficult to arrest. Finally, after the relationship is on the verge of total collapse, the participants manage to reverse the direction of the relationship patterns. Through active participation in marriage enrichment programs, self-examination, and a job change, the couple is able to begin building progressive spirals. And because they recognize some of the techniques for altering spirals, they can help other couples in their counseling programs to check the ever-damaging course of regressive relationships. Quite clearly, other dyads experience similar stages. The employer-employee dyad or any dyadic pairing that exists for a length of time, will fluctuate between regressive and progressive stages.

This short description of one marital dyad illustrates a number of central points concerning all dyadic relationships. To begin with, dyadic relationships fluctuate between varying stages of progressive and regressive spirals. The actions of each participant either accelerate a spiral in progress or provide pressure so that the direction of the spiral will change. All spirals have limits, and once the critical limit is reached and the spiral is not reversed, the relationship will suffer so much strain that it will dissolve.

Such a course, however, is not inevitable. Participants can and do check the course of a spiral by altering it. A regressive spiral, for instance, may be altered for a number of reasons. As Waller and Hill [314] noted, for a marital pair engaged in a regressive conflict, support from friends, the desire to make the marriage work, and even sexual relations can be used to alter the course of a regressive spiral. Obviously in other kinds of dyads, the reasons for limiting regressiveness are different. As an employee, for instance, your desire to keep your job can prevent you from engaging in open verbal conflict with your employer.

Even though dyadic relationships are continually changing, they can have a predominant mode. Some romantic pairs function in regressive spirals more often than in positive ones, and vice versa. And concomitantly, a relationship that appears stable is one in which

---

*I am indebted to James Click for suggesting the term *critical limit*.

the fluctuations of relationship are less intense than in others. But in any event, no relationship can remain at the same degree of progressiveness or regressiveness indefinitely.

PARADOXES

Paradoxes occur when a communication is self-contradictory. For example, a friend looks you right in the eye and says, "I hate you!" Then, just when you are trying to recover, he adds, "But you must remember I always lie." Your friend has placed you in a paradoxical situation; he has made a statement which is simultaneously a statement that contradicts itself [248]. The difficulty arises because the statement (1) asserts something and (2) asserts something about its own assertion. In addition, the two assertions are mutually exclusive [330].

Paradoxes are prevalent. Once their basic form is understood, their existence is easily recognized. For instance, study the statement within the box in Fig. 5–3.

> Every statement in
> this box is false.

Fig. 5-3   A paradoxical statement.

Is the statement true or false? "If the assertion is true, then by its own evidence it is not true; and if the assertion is false, then that tells us that what is being said must be true" [41]. Such classic paradoxes are often used in logic classes to demonstrate the theory of types, that statements occur at many levels. A statement and a statement about a statement are obviously at different levels. Even if you never attend a logic class, you may encounter variations of the classic paradoxes. You might be driving down the street, look at the bumper of the car in front of you, and see a sticker proclaiming

> THIS IS NOT A BUMPER STICKER

Then, just as you are trying to restore some mental equilibrium, you encounter a road sign proclaiming the following.

```
IGNORE THIS SIGN
```

Paradoxes occur in everyday communication as well. Dan Greenburg supplies the following as a sampling of the fare a Jewish mother has to offer.

> Florence, what have you done to your hair. It looks like you're wearing a wig?
> I am—all my hair fell out!
> Oh, listen, it looks so natural I'd never have known [110].*

Greenburg also offers this advice to the woman who wants to be a successful Jewish mother. When you talk to your son, "don't let him know you fainted twice in the supermarket from fatigue (but make sure he knows you're not letting him know)" [110].

Other variations of paradoxes crop up in conversations from time to time. The wife who says to her meek husband, "Damn it, dominate me!" is placing him in a paradox. If he obeys and dominates her, it is because he responded to her domination of him. Whenever a dyadic participant says things like the following, the partner has been placed in a paradox:

> "Don't think about me." (parting lovers)
>
> "I always lie." (your friend, the philosophy major)
>
> "I want you to disagree with everything I say." (professor to student)
>
> "Tell me what to do so I can be independent." (client to therapist)
>
> "Don't ever listen to me." (your mother)
>
> "I can't tell you that I love you because then you'll leave me." (your anxious lover)
>
> "I think you should quit school, but it's not my place to say so." (your friend)

---

*While not fitting the exact form of a classic paradox, the essential element of denial of the initial statement is present.

While paradoxes are readily spotted once the basic form is recognized, some people are able to recognize them in their own behavior. Golas [104] says, "I am playing the game of refusing pointless games, which may be the most pointless of all." Some astute Harlem resident also demonstrated his understanding of paradoxes. "You can't be free if someone else lets you be free" [237]. The next time you attend a party, try this on one of your friends who is not initiated into the intricacies of paradoxes:

> In a small village there is a barber who shaves all the men who do not shave themselves. When he gets down to the last man, the barber, does he shave him? [330].

Paradoxes can be fun, but beyond that they make a serious point about human communication. Communication can occur on more than one level. The first two levels are (1) communication and (2) metacommunication (communication about communication).* When these two levels agree, such as someone saying, "I always tell the truth," there is no paradox. But when one's metacommunication denies the communication, a paradox exists.

The habitual use of paradoxes can sometimes be a sign of a communication pathology. We all attempt to control relationships, but if we control them while sending the metacommunication denying that we are controlling, we might be indicating "symptomatic behavior" [113]. The "double-bind" hypothesis deals specifically with these communicative paradoxes. The necessary conditions producing the double-bind are:

1. Two persons, one of whom is the victim.
2. Repeated experience so that the double-bind becomes an habitual expectation.
3. A primary negative injunction.
4. A secondary injunction conflicting with the first injunction, but at a more abstract level. Like the primary injunction, the second threatens punishment.

---

*Note that these levels are similar to the levels of perspectives introduced in the last chapter (direct perspective, metaperspective, meta-metaperspective).

5. A tertiary negative injunction prohibiting the victim from escaping from the field.

6. A victim who begins to see the entire universe in double-bind patterns [20].

A double-bind, therefore, is a paradox. Double-binds are often created when the verbal message is contradicted by the nonverbal message [261]. When the mother says, "Go son, be independent of me and make your own life," and then reels backward due to her "heart attack," she has put the boy in a double-bind.

Theoretically, repeated exposure to double-binds produces schizophrenia [20]. The evidence of this, however, is not totally convincing [264a]. In fact, double-binds are quite easily found in cases where no schizophrenia is present. For instance, watch what happens when a small child falls and scrapes a knee. The parent will commonly cuddle the sobbing child and say, "Oh, now, that doesn't hurt you." The child receives two conflicting messages—the hug supports the idea he was hurt, but the verbal injunction denies the hurt. And importantly, the child cannot escape the field; he has to try and deal with the double-bind as best he can. The research by Berger [27] was an inquiry into the double-binds that adults saw themselves placed in as children. He constructed lists of double-bind statements and asked schizophrenics, mental patients who were not schizophrenics, ward attendants, and college students the extent to which their mothers typically made such statements. The schizophrenics attributed more double-bind statements to their mothers than did those in any of the other groups. While there were problems in recalling events because of the selectivity of remembering [264a], the data are certainly interesting. While it has been demonstrated that schizophrenics engage in unusual communicative behaviors, the contributing causes to these behaviors are not yet clearly isolated. The double-bind hypothesis is a fascinating one because it pinpoints dyadic transactions as the core of the problem. To this date, however, there are many unresolved questions relating to the double-bind hypothesis. It is not clear, for instance, what the relationships are between all the possible types of double-binds [264a]. And more importantly, the extent to which double-binds exist in "normal" transactions is yet to be determined. Furthermore, while the original formulation of the hypothesis specified that disturbed individuals could not effectively deal with the metacommunication level, Loeff [172] found that disturbed individuals were more influenced by the metacommunicative level of messages. And most important of all, the perception each dyadic participant has of a double-bind is crucial. It may well be that in close friendships and other stable dyadic pairings, occasional use of double-binds actually reinforces the relationship.

Double-binds have actually been used for therapeutic purposes. One of the more provocative views of psychotherapy is that it is designed to "challenge the patient's false and neurotic assumptions so that the more he holds to them, the more he finds himself in a double-bind" [319]. Haley [113] advanced the view that all the schools of psychotherapy have one central commonality, that of placing the patient in a paradoxical situation. For instance, when a patient requests the therapist to tell him what to do, he is defining the relationship as one in which he is not in control [112]. The therapist, therefore, can alter the client's behavior by reversing the situation, by placing the patient in paradoxes. As an example, the client knows the relationship is voluntary, yet the therapist makes regular attendance necessary. The patient is also blamed and not blamed at the same time. The patient is given the message that whatever the matter is, it is not his fault. Yet psychotherapy is based on the premise that the patient can control his behavior because that's why he is there for treatment. Additional similar paradoxes hopefully set the patient on the course to a better life [113]. Seeing psychotherapy within this framework creates a few more twists in the rope of the logic of relationships.*

In summary, paradoxes occur when a statement asserts something, when the statement asserts something about its own assertion, and when these two assertions are mutually exclusive. In dyadic

---

*For your friends who replied to the case of the barber in the village that it was impossible, a paradox, give them this problem which does have a solution. You are a prisoner held by two guards, one who always lies and one who always tells the truth. You have one chance to gain your freedom. You have to identify which one of two doors leading to your cell is unlocked and which one is locked. You can only ask one question of one guard. If you don't ask the question, or ask it and then guess incorrectly which door is unlocked, you will be killed. If you guess correctly, you will be set free. You can't guess the correct door by any other method than asking a question. (For example, you can't go try the doors or see which one the guards use.) What is your one question?

transactions, paradoxes occur in the form of double-binds, a term coined by Bateson. The double-bind hypothesis states that prolonged exposure to communicative paradoxes without the opportunity to withdraw can produce communicative disturbances in the victim. Whatever future research and theorizing discover about the use and misuse of communicative paradoxes, they remain one of the most fascinating examples of relational intricacies.

DO-LOOPS

A communication do-loop [344] is very similar to a paradox. Both have as their essential elements (1) a communication and (2) a communication about the communication (metacommunication). A paradox exists when the metacommunication contradicts or denies the communication. In do-loops, the metacommunication sends the analysis to higher and higher levels of abstraction, such that meta-metacommunication and other levels are present.

The human mind has the ability to metacommunicate, which is self-reflexive when turned internally. The mind can turn upon itself and, using its processes, examine its own processes. As noted in the second chapter, self-reflexiveness can sometimes pose problems. For an individual who simply experiences life and never reflects on it, do-loops pose no problem. But when one "goes beyond simple experiencing and making statements about his experiencing to new levels where he thinks about the way he thinks about things," do-loops set in [344]. Do-loops are situations of "infinite regress," a spiraling to higher and higher levels of abstraction. The process of self-analysis can end up just like two mirrors, facing each other and endlessly reflecting the other's reflections. A do-loop is an expanding cycle of reflexiveness that "continually tries to encompass itself, a kind of Alice-down-the-rabbit-hole spiral" [344]. Do-loops share similarities with paradoxes (the shifting between levels) and with spirals (the ever-increasing nature of the reflexiveness).

Do-loops can occur for a variety of reasons. One of the most common is because an individual tends to rigidly apply labels to his behaviors and then begins reacting to the labels. If a man sees himself as generous and selfless, but ends up taking a trip instead of giving the vacation money to his brother's widow for his hospital expenses, "he misconstrues the meaning of such an act as indicating once and for all that he is a tight, selfish, and money-grabbing person . . ." [335].

> A kind of rigid logic then takes over in the mind of the helpless victim and starts him thinking what he is and what he should be, the ways in which he can look like what he should be, how he can *try* to actually *be* what he should be, and perhaps mistakenly, thinks he is not; he develops new and more complicated ways of thinking about himself and the world; he becomes compelled to block out whole areas of his most basic experiencing; he becomes frightened of finding out who he *really* is; his mind goes beyond simple experiencing and making statements about his experiencing to new levels where he thinks about the way he thinks about things; and it is not long before he finds himself entertaining and rejecting the same ideas over and over again, caught in circles and eddies of reasoning he is incapable of getting out of [344].

Woodman's solution to do-loops is for the individual to free himself from his rigid set of categories. By giving himself the "permission" to feel and experience and to follow those feelings regardless of how illogical or unreasonable they seem, the pattern of infinite regression can be halted. Put simply, one must try to discard rigid categories when they create do-loops; one must experience openly and let in new meanings for one's behavior.

Do-loops caused by one's self-reflexiveness going into deeper and deeper levels are a communication situation that Frankl has also dealt with. His psychiatry has focused on individuals who perpetually are caught in do-loops. In a typical case, the burden of "unavoidable unhappiness" of a person is increased by "unhappiness about being unhappy" [332]. Or take the case of a patient who cannot sleep at night. His fear of the sleeplessness results in a "hyperintention to fall asleep, which, in turn, incapacitates the patient to do so" [93]. Frankl's logotherapy (meaning therapy) is used to break the self-fulfilling do-loops and free the patient of the concerns. The technique is quite simple. One engages in "paradoxical intention"; you try to do the very thing you are trying to change [93]. If you can't break the spiraling effects of unhappiness, you try to be as unhappy as possible. If your problem is sleeplessness, you apply paradoxical intention and, upon going to bed, try to stay awake. One client had a problem

with sweating when others were around, and, of course, his anticipation of it caused him to sweat all the more. Frankl advised him to
deliberately show people how much he could sweat, and the do-loop
was broken.

Woodman's and Frankl's solutions to do-loops are quite similar.
One has to change the meaning for his behavior. It is the person's
view of his own behavior that sets up the do-loop. So by engaging in
opposite behavior so you can't keep applying your old meanings, or
by letting yourself experience things without rigidly classifying them,
the do-loops can be broken.

A do-loop is an intrapersonal process; it occurs solely within the
thinking processes of one person. Do-loops do, however, have an impact on one's dyadic transactions. In its most extreme form, it is a
completely debilitating form of self-reflexiveness. One becomes so
engaged in his intrapersonal transactions that he cannot respond fully
or appropriately to the dyadic partner. Look at some of the intriguing
examples of do-loops that R. D. Laing supplied in his best-selling
book, *Knots* [158]. They demonstrate how one's thinking processes
can affect a relationship.

JILL: You put me in the wrong

JACK: I am not putting you in the wrong

JILL: You put me in the wrong for thinking you put me in the
wrong

. . . .

There must be something the matter with him
        because he would not be acting as he does
            unless there was
        therefore he is acting as he is
        because there is something the matter with him
He does not think there is anything the matter with him
because
        one of things that is
        the matter with him
        is that he does not think that there is anything
        the matter with him

Therefore
>we have to help him realize that,
>the fact that he does not think there is anything
>the matter with him
>is one of the things that is
>the matter with him

. . . .

JILL

I don't respect myself
I can't respect anyone who respects me.
I can only respect someone who does not respect me.

I respect Jack
because he does not respect me

I despise Tom
because he does not despise me

Only a despicable person
can respect someone as despicable as me

I cannot love someone I despise

Since I love Jack
I cannot believe he loves me

What proof can he give?

When Jill is in such a do-loop, Jack cannot give any proof of his love. As a result, her preoccupation with herself blocks an appropriate communicative exchange with Jack. Sometimes, however, it is beneficial to a dyadic pair when one of the partners is caught in a limited do-loop. Take the case of a marital dyad from the wife's point of view:

>"I would cheat on my husband only with a man I considered worthy.
>I would never consider a man worthy who was the type that would run around with a married woman."

Such a do-loop, especially if both partners are caught in one like it, could have beneficial effects on a marital dyad. The effects of do-loops on dyadic transactions of all types have yet to be investigated. It may be that a detailed study of participants' do-loops could isolate some of the reasons behind faulty dyadic transactions. And as a result of providing solutions to do-loops, some dyadic transactions could be strengthened.*

Do-loops are characterized by uncontrolled self-reflexiveness. The levels of thinking keep cycling back until the mind cannot logically escape from the entangling web. Such logical intricacies provide interesting dilemmas. For example, if a psychologist or communication expert could perfectly predict your behavior, the prediction will be correct only if he doesn't tell you of his prediction. If he tells you, he will find himself in an endless regression "to allow for the effects of allowing for the effects of allowing for the effects indefinitely" [128].

SUMMARY

Because communication involves participants who respond to each other, dyadic relationships can take strange turns. Self-fulfilling prophecies occur because another responds to the meaning one has in such a way as to validate it. Spirals happen when each person's behavior feeds energy into an ongoing system that further increases its basic nature, whether progressive or regressive. Paradoxes and do-loops exist because of the unique abilities humans have to communicate at different levels. When the levels contradict, a paradox is present; when each level forces the analysis to an even deeper level, the infinite regressiveness of do-loops is experienced. All of these phenomena share one common characteristic: They are intricate relationships formed by the combination and, in some cases, acceleration of the dyadic participants' perspectives.

---

*Are you still caught in prison from the example given earlier? Here is how you could get out. You simply ask one guard, "If I asked the other guard if the door on the right was unlocked, what would he say?" Regardless of which guard you asked, the liar or the truth teller, if he says, "No," the answer is yes; if he says, "Yes," the answer is no. The liar will lie about the true answer and the truthful guard will tell the truth about the lie.

Chapter 6
Improving Dyadic Relationships

Try an experiment. During the next week, keep a mental note of how many times your acquaintances bring up topics of interpersonal communication — the wife who complains that her husband doesn't spend enough time with her, the student who mentions that professor X is a crashing bore, or the close friend who tries to decide whether or not to get married. All of these and other problems focus on human communication, namely, how the relationship between two or more people is progressing. If you try the experiment, you will notice that people are often concerned with how they might improve their relationships.

There are numerous possible solutions to communication problems. One can try everything from hypnosis to a nude marathon as a relationship aid. Current books available will instruct you on everything from constructive fighting to being an effective parent. This last chapter is also addressed to improving relationships. It will focus on things you can do to alter and hopefully improve your dyadic relationships. It is a "shopping list" of some select possibilities that you may find useful. If only one of the suggestions aids you in improving an important relationship, your time has been well spent. The discussion focuses on two levels: (1) improvements brought about by some action on your part, a behavior change, or even a new way of thinking, and (2) improvements brought about by more general aspects of a particular relationship. Keep in mind that improvements can be made in any relationship, not just in those with serious problems.

PERSONAL IMPROVEMENTS

It has been stressed repeatedly that dyadic communication is transactional in nature. Any one change in the system reverberates throughout the system; alteration of one person's behavior produces changes in other areas. One of the quickest ways, therefore, to alter any relationship is for one person to change his behavior. If you and a close friend are slowly drifting apart, a phone call to him inviting him to your house may serve to solidify the relationship. All too often when people encounter difficulties in a dyadic relationship, they try to change the other person rather than themselves. It's difficult to look at yourself first, but that is where the change can be made most productively.

Analyze Your Needs.   One way to improve your dyadic relationship is to analyze your own needs, because one of the pathways to self-improvement is self-knowledge. Unfortunately, self-knowledge is difficult for most people to achieve. One has to "stand outside oneself" and look in. The task is to try to understand what one's own needs are and then see if a particular relationship fulfills them. Glasser notes that we all have "the need to love and be loved and the need to feel that we are worthwhile to ourselves and others" [102]. These basic needs are fulfilled by one's involvement with at least one other person.

It is in our involvement with another that we determine if our needs are being met. And obviously, different needs are important in different situations. The author recalls very vividly his early years as a graduate student. I wanted to feel significant and worthwhile; that my existence made some difference. For the first few years I was very frustrated. My needs to be included by professors and have an impact on the profession were not fulfilled. Fortunately for me, I later found myself in a situation with two professors who treated me with respect. When my needs for inclusion were being met, it made a world of difference to me. If you are at all like me, when you are transacting with another it is easy to determine if your needs for that situation are being met. How do you feel about yourself in that situation? When you "fall in love," for instance, you feel good about yourself when you are with that person. If you feel significant and worthwhile when at your job, the demands you place on that situation are being met.

Once you can analyze yourself with respect to a particular relationship, possible remedies for unfulfilled needs may be close at hand. Knowing that you like to dominate the other person in a romance can prompt you to choose a marital partner who wants you to be domineering. Knowing you want to feel that you contribute to the world can prompt you to seek relationships wherein coworkers will respond to your efforts. Knowing you become morose if left alone can prompt you to seek situations where a lot of people are present. You can, in short, maximize the pleasure of being alive by choosing situations and relationships that are consistent with your basic needs as you understand them. We are, after all, responsible for our own lives. We cannot demand or dictate that others should make us happy. But we can select situations and people with whom we are happy. The really difficult part comes in fulfilling our needs in such a way "that does not deprive others of the ability to fulfill their needs" [106]. Your needs are fulfilled or frustrated with respect to others, and because of the obligation you have to yourself, you have an obligation to them.

Check Your Perceptions.   This is a perceptual world. We all react on the basis of the meanings that people and events have for us. The meanings, of course, are individualized. If you say to one friend, "I disagree," it is taken as a positive expression of your feelings, something that is valued in the relationship. Yet if you say to a second friend, "I disagree," he may interpret it as an attempt to deflate his ego. The meaning each person attaches to "I disagree" will structure his response back to you.

We all attach meanings to the events and people around us. And in order to make sense out of our world, we develop sets or categories to use in new situations. For instance, if you once met a homosexual who was effeminate in his behavior, you might easily develop the perceptual set that homosexuals are effeminate. The next time you are introduced to a man who has some effeminate behaviors, you are likely to conclude that he is a homosexual. He may or may not be a homosexual; the point is that you used a perceptual set to evaluate him. Your prearranged category system was ready and waiting to be used. Perceptual sets are used so frequently that we usually do not even notice that we use them until the perception we had is blatantly disproved. As a college professor, I used to strongly believe that the best students in a class were those who spoke up and contributed to class discussion. It was not until I began receiving superior papers from reticent students that I recognized my perceptual set. All along I "knew" I was right, until I was proved wrong.

Look at Fig. 6–1. Which items are added incorrectly?

$$2 + 2 = 4$$
$$8 + 4 = 12$$
$$10 + 3 = 1$$
$$2 + 4 = 6$$
$$9 + 5 = 2$$
$$5 + 2 = 7$$
$$1 + 8 = 9$$

Fig. 6–1   Addition problem.

Are any items added incorrectly? You probably saw incorrect addition in the cases of $10 + 3 = 1$ and $9 + 5 = 2$. You used the perceptual set of usual addition rules to tell that these two were incorrect. But by using an alternative perception of the rules of addition, each addition is entirely correct. The numbers you are adding are on the face of a clock. When you reach twelve you begin over again at one. Using those rules for organization, $8 + 4 = 12$, $10 + 3 = 1$, and likewise, $9 + 5 = 2$. All the additions are correct. When faced with new situations, we invoke perceptual sets that have worked in past situations. It is done so automatically that we do not even notice it. In the case above, most of us immediately call forth the addition rules we have used all our lives.

In dyadic relationships, perceptual sets have the same utility— letting you organize information — and the same liability, possibly not being appropriate in a particular situation. One insurmountable barrier, however, is present. There is usually no "true" or "correct" interpretation that you can check your perception against to test its accuracy. The best you can do is to see how others perceive the situation. If you have an acquaintance you feel cannot be trusted, some validity is added to your perception if you discover that others see him the same way. However, if you check your perceptions only with your close friends, you can expect similar perceptions. It rarely helps to check your perceptions with a friend—no doubt you are friends because you share many common perceptions.

Identify the Perceptual Set.   Recalling the addition problem presented above, you had to identify the perceptual set you were using before you could open yourself to new interpretations. The same is true when dealing with people—you have to identify your perceptual sets before you can alter them. It is when you *know* you are right about another person that you are in perceptual trouble. Self-fulfilling prophecies come into operation, and the way you perceive someone becomes the truth. If your perceptual set is so strong that you cannot identify it, then you begin operating like some of the characters in *One Flew Over the Cuckoo's Nest*—"It's the truth even if it didn't happen." It is not until the original definition of a person or situation is identified that it can be abandoned. "Only when the original assumption is questioned and a new definition of the situation introduced, does the consequent flow of events give the lie to the

assumption. Only then does the belief no longer father the reality"
[196].

In dyadic transactions in which participants' perceptual sets are
too rigid and not open to any alteration, communication difficulties
are bound to arise sooner or later. As a relationship goes through
changes, the perceptions must, of necessity, keep pace if the relationship is to maintain harmony. As Ruesch [246] notes, excessive
rigidity can lead to communication breakdown. The mutual frame of
reference that two participants supply will require some changes as
time passes. McGuire [187] goes so far as to note that mental patients
superimpose their models (perceptual sets) on the world rather than
use them as a basis for interacting with the world. Each perceptual set
should be capable of updating at some point in time.* Even in an
intrapersonal sense, rigid categorization leads to difficulties. As noted
in the previous chapter, people become caught in do-loops because
they rigidly apply perceptual sets to their own behavior.

There are obviously no foolproof guidelines you can use to de-
tect if your perceptual sets are resisting any change because they are
too rigidly held. One guideline may be this: If you are finding fault
with another, namely, judging, evaluating, and disapproving of him,
you have already lost the battle of appropriate perception of an
event. Certainly at a minimum, the tendency to judge and "approve
or disapprove the statement of the other" is a prominent barrier to
effective dyadic communication [235]. Another guideline may be that
if you react to your *concept* of a person rather than to the person
himself, you are using a perceptual set. If the classifications you place
him in carry a strong meaning for you, you are calling forth perceptual sets that may be inappropriate. Is your reaction triggered by the
fact he is black, is a student, is rich, or has a Ph.D.? Whatever category the person is in, if you respond to him on that basis, you are
using a perceptual set that may be too rigid.

Of course, identifying a perceptual set and leaving it open to
change is sometimes risky. You may end up changing many aspects
of your own life. Romey describes in poetic form how a change in

---

*Ruesch [246] also notes the dangers from too much flexibility in perceptual
sets. One needs to have some system for organizing incoming information.
The usual case, however, is having too rigid a system rather than none at all.

perception of the self can lead to other alterations. His message is applicable to us all, regardless of our chosen role.

A Warning

If you change your perception of your
Role as a teacher, you may find
The rest of your life changing, too!
Working at becoming a whole human being and sharing
Your perceptions, fears, joys, and loves
Openly is risky business
But the progess makes me feel good
Much of the time [237].

Seek Out Other Perceptions.   Once you have identified a perceptual set as being inappropriate for a new situation because of its rigidity, how can you alter it? Most importantly, you need new options to choose from. *All* perceptions of an event or person are only partial views. Therefore, give yourself the opportunity to absorb other points of view. Once you realize that every judgment you make of another is a product of your perception transacting with an event, it can actually be exciting to seek out other perceptions.

As noted earlier, try to not collect the perceptions of your close friends; they will probably not perceive things differently than you do. Find someone who has a different relationship with the person than you do. For instance, if you are a college student and you have a professor that you dislike because he makes you feel uneasy, a friend likely will agree and say, "Yes, that's right. He is out to get students and I feel uneasy, too." But what might happen if you talked to another professor, one who is a close friend of the professor who makes you feel uneasy? He will undoubtedly give you a different viewpoint, an option to select from. It may be that your professor deliberately makes students uneasy as a way to motivate them, or he may not even know that the students feel threatened by him. The possibilities are endless.

One of the best things you can do to improve a dyadic relationship is to seek out the perception of the other person involved. From our point of view, we often cannot understand why others do what they do. But "from the point of view of his role-identities, and his perception of opportunities—his behavior is eminently reasonable" [185]. Put another way, *people have reasons.** Ichheiser expands on this principle by explaining its utility for perception:

> . . . if other people react to certain situations which are to them highly real but are not visible to us from our point of view, we fail to understand why they behave as they do even though in terms of those invisible factors their behavior is perfectly understandable and "reasonable." What really happens is that, not being aware of our own social blindness, we misinterpret (and usually denounce) their behavior as unreasonable, or abnormal or aggressive [132].

Once exposed to the other person's perspectives on a situation, your own perception can be altered. As is usually the case, each person's perceptions will undergo some changes, since neither single perception by itself can possibly encompass the event. And interestingly enough, taking the time to understand another's reality does not destroy your own, but can be used to supplement it.†

Perceptual sets can also be altered by other techniques. One is to internalize the premise of uniqueness [115]. Knowing that no things are alike—no two snowflakes, no two blades of grass, and certainly no two people. We are not even identical in small respects. The presumption that no two fingerprints are exactly the same has yet to be disproved, even though there are three billion people in the world [115]. With approximately ten fingers each, that's a lot of uniqueness! Is it any wonder, then, that when we respond to another on the basis of some very general category—age, sex, religion, color, or occupation—that our perceptual set may be inaccurate?

The perceptions you have of an event and of your behavior are closely allied. You can change your perception by changing your be-

---

*The author first heard this phrase used by Robert Sallery. It serves as a continual reminder to check the other's perceptions of a situation.

†It is often useful to assess the full range of perspectives—direct, meta, and meta-meta (see Chapter 4). Also, it is quite true that the joint product of any two perceptions is not a complete view, but it yields more information than one viewpoint alone.

havior and your behavior by changing your perception.* As noted earlier, your liking (perception) of someone will change if you perform a favor for them. And likewise, once your perception changes, new behaviors are possible. The author was able to quit smoking ("It's easy to quit; I've done it fifteen times.") by redefining it. Once I began to see smoking as a habit that made someone else rich by me ruining my lungs, I could stop. By changing either perceptions or behavior, other changes will appear. As you add new information about the other person or give that person new information about yourself by changing in some way, the dyadic relationship will be affected. As you begin to relate to someone as a unique person rather than just a representative of a category, that person will respond by changing his behavior, too. One of the quickest and most effective ways to improve a dyadic relationship is for you to undergo a personal behavioral change by altering your perceptual sets.

Confirm the Other.   If you are involved in a dyad that makes you uncomfortable or that lacks that "special something" of a good relationship, another road to personal improvement is to transact appropriately, to confirm the needs the other person has in the relationship. By doing so, you open him up so that he can fully respond to you. For until the other individual can feel fulfilled in the relationship, he may not be able to relate to your needs. By meeting the other's needs, you free him to be able to meet yours.

Not all communication transactions can be characterized as confirming the interlocking responses of the participants. Put simply, a response may not be appropriate (relevant or clear to the other) [277a]. Various descriptions have been made of responses in transactions that do not confirm the other's existence. Piaget [229] noted that children often engage in parallel play; they are in close physical proximity, yet play independently of each other. Similarly, "collective monologues" occur, wherein each person continues his own conversation independently of the other's response. Two conversations occur under the guise of one.

Ruesch has spent considerable time identifying a form of inappropriateness that he labels "tangential feedback." The tangential re-

---

*Haney [115] offers some specific suggestions applicable to our personal lives and business decisions about how to alter "blinders," or perceptual sets.

sponse is one that deprives the sender the pleasure of being understood. If the response does not fit the initial statement in terms of language, content, or emotional commitment, it is tangential. By not responding appropriately, the receiver "makes a bid for control by launching another statement which he expects to be acknowledged in turn" [246]. Wenburg and Wilmot [334] labeled this type of tangential response the "mother-in-law syndrome." In this case, the inappropriate response occurs because a young man's mother-in-law continually switches topics on him so rapidly that he cannot keep pace. She fails to confirm his communication attempts. Ruesch classifies the tangential response as one type of disturbed message. He very aptly captures the essence of all disturbed messages by his poem:

Too much,
Too little,
Too early,
Too late,
At the wrong place,
Is the disturbed message's fate [246].

In the terminology used here, a nondisturbing or appropriate response would confirm the other person, and a disturbing or inappropriate response would disconfirm the other person. As Watzlawick, Beavin, and Jackson [330] demonstrate, you can respond to another by accepting, rejecting, or denying. Whether you are accepting or rejecting the other's ideas, you are still confirming his presence, which is an appropriate response. Denial of the other person's existence is a disconfirming response. Confirming responses are those that acknowledge the other, clarify what he said, give a supportive response, agree about content, and express positive feelings [277a]. Conversely, a disconfirming response is one that is irrelevant, tangential, impersonal, incoherent, incongruent, or impervious. The appendix lists full definitions and samples of each of these types of responses.

What effects do each of these responses have on individuals? It has been fairly well documented that disconfirming responses occur with considerable frequency in transactions between disturbed individuals [156, 244, 245, 246, 247, 282, 330, 335, 340]. On the other hand, transactions within small groups also manifest disconfirming responses, but to a lesser degree [277a]. Undoubtedly, a prolonged use of disconfirming responses will begin to damage any dyadic relationship. Lederer and Jackson [165] suggest that disconfirming responses can literally drive one's spouse crazy.

One can read over Lederer and Jackson's list of destructive behaviors or consider the types of disconfirming responses as a baseline for evaluating one's own behavior. When all is said and done, that is the crucial issue. Do you continually disconfirm your dyadic partner? Do you leave conversations without really learning anything about the other or what the other has said? Do people always become quiet and withdrawn in your presence? Do changes occur in yourself after a communication transaction, or is the influence only one way? Do you always feel compelled to "prove yourself" to others? Can you accurately remember what the other participant said, or do you only remember your own contributions? Did the other person play a role in influencing the flow of events, or did you dictate everything that happened? In sum, do you engage in behaviors that tend to confirm the other person's uniqueness, that increase his sense of self-worth?

The very best way to begin improving a dyadic relationship is to undergo personal improvements. These improvements can range from analyzing your needs, to checking your perceptions, to confirming the other person. In all cases, your own behavior has a tremendous impact on the dyadic relationship.

RELATIONSHIP IMPROVEMENTS

All the personal improvements suggested above are designed to achieve one goal, the improvement of dyadic relationships. Whereas one avenue to change is personal modification, another is relationship modification, the focus here being on the joint product of the two individuals' behavior. This section will offer suggestions about how to analyze a relationship, what characterizes a good relationship, why rules are important, and how to help direct the course a relationship takes.

Analyze the Relationship.   One of the most useful things to do in any relationship is to be aware of its basic nature. Whether you are trying to improve a teacher-student, friendship, generation, or romantic-pair relationship, some basic principles hold true, namely (1) relationships change and (2) relationships require attention.

First, all relationships undergo change. Try as we might, it is impossible to "freeze" a relationship at a given stage. For instance, the excitement that comes with first meeting and getting to know a romantic partner cannot continue to exist to the same degree. As you come to know each other, you respond differently to the relationship, thus effecting change. If you try to preserve the initial excitement by "putting the relationship on the shelf" for a while, you will be disappointed. Change in participants and therefore in relationships is inevitable. "The relationship must undergo metamorphosis at each major turning point in the personal career of each participant" [185]. If the participants are not willing to accept the inevitability of change, difficulties arise. In marital dyads, for instance, many spouses interpret change in the other partner (and therefore change in the relationship) as a betrayal of trust [165]. If the participants change but are unwilling to accept change in their relationship, the relationship will "fade away or be destroyed" [185]. The first step, therefore, in analyzing any relationship is to realize that relationship change is inevitable.

Not only do relationships change, in their formative stages the changes are sequential. Altman and Taylor's [6] theory of social penetration specifically traces the development of interpersonal relationships. Put succinctly, social transactions proceed "gradually and systematically from superficial to intimate topics." As a result, incorrect timing of behaviors, such as revealing very personal information on a first meeting, disrupts the pattern of slow increments and puts strain on the relationship.* One's behaviors have to be attuned to the other's expectations. Especially in the case of self-disclosure, when one person honestly shares personal information with another, the timing of the remarks is crucial. The self-disclosure occurs incrementally over time, and as one person increases his disclosure, so does the other person [222].† From the transactional perspective, each person's disclosing behavior is in part a function of the other's, and disclosure at too early a stage is inappropriate. It should be clearly recognized that all continuing dyadic relationships progress through stages [6].

---

*The notable exception is the case in which the other person is a stranger with whom no subsequent transaction is expected [222].

†Jourard calls this the "dyadic effect."

Second, relationships require attention. Because relationships undergo change, the participants need to give their attention to those changes. A romantic pair that marries and has children soon discovers that the old assumptions about the relationship need to be reexamined. Even if no dramatic change occurs in a relationship, attention is required for maintenance of a good relationship. In the case of a romantic pair, participants have to *keep working on their relationship until the day they die* [165]. If we all worked on our relationships as much as we did our jobs, we would have a richer emotional life. To assume that your relationship will maintain itself is very naive; it requires time and work. If you pay no attention to your important dyadic relationships, they will fade away.

The Good Relationship.   When one tries to improve a relationship, one presumes there is some goal that can be more fully attained. Our dyadic relationships obviously serve different functions for us. We expect to achieve different goals in different dyads. Relationships with spouse, friend, and relative typically serve goals that, while they may overlap, are not the same. Furthermore, one marital dyad may not have the same function as another marital dyad. What is important is the function the dyadic relationship serves for the particular participants.

A good relationship is one that serves the functions for which it was formed [25]. If two people get married in order to increase their joint income and expect and receive little emotional satisfaction, the marriage is a "good" one. While someone else may observe the marriage and conclude, "I don't see why they stay married. They seem to have little emotional commitment," one is applying his own goals to their marriage. The two participants may be perfectly satisfied with the relationship.

Bennis, et al. [25] have suggested an interesting classification for the primary functions that relationships serve. Type *A* relationships are formed for emotional-expressive purposes. Emotional-expressive relationships are formed for the purpose of fulfilling emotional needs. Typical dyads in which these functions are prominent are romantic and friendship pairs. Type *B* relationships are confirmatory; they exist in order to establish reality. As a participant in this type of relationship, you receive (1) information about yourself from the reflected appraisals of others, and (2) information about the situation, your perceptions and definitions of the situation being validated by others.* When confirmation is not forthcoming, there is a lack of consensus about reality. Confirmation is obviously crucial in all dyadic pairs, but especially so in the dyads typified by the more personable qualities of friendship, romantic, and generation pairs.

The primary function of type C relationships is change-influence. Some goal is desired, and change or progress toward that goal is the basis for evaluation of the dyad. Typically, the goal has to do with another person, as in an aider-aided dyad. The teacher, the psychiatrist, or the coach has the role of producing change in the other participant. As a result, attaining the goal is a sign of success. In instrumental relationships, type D, the goal is a task; the relationship is formed in order to produce or create. Joining together in a business relationship is one of the simplest examples of this type of relationship often found in superior-subordinate dyads.

The basis for a relationship can shift over time. A teacher-student dyad may begin as a change-influence or instrumental relationship and shift to an emotional-expressive one, the two ultimately getting married. In fact, if the participants want it to, the basis for a relationship may shift many times. As long as the relationship fulfills the functions the participants want, it is a good relationship. However, when a shift of functions occurs that one or both participants do not accept, necessary adjustments must be made. The classic case of a romantic relationship leading to marriage, then, being transformed over time into an instrumental relationship is a case in point. If one person still wants emotional-expressive functions and the other only wants task-oriented behaviors, adjustments are required in order to bring satisfaction to both participants.

Relationships become exceptional and extremely satisfying when they exceed the minimal expectations of the participants [25]. When the behaviors go above and beyond what the role requires, the relationship moves to a new elevated plane. As a teacher, I find that when a student and I become good friends, the relationship becomes something special to us both. The relationship may have begun as

---

*Earlier in this chapter, confirmation of the other was stressed. In all dyads that extend beyond initial encounters, unless confirmation is received, other functions cannot be fulfilled.

instrumental or change-influence based, but then moves to a confirmatory or emotional-expressive relationship. In a word, it becomes more personal. When the romantic partner also becomes a friend, the student a colleague (or the professor a friend), and the employee a committed worker, minimal expectations are far surpassed. A good relationship is one that fulfills its functions; a bad one does not. And a superior one exceeds the minimal expectations set for it.

Relationship Rules. When dyadic participants enter into a relationship, they each develop a perspective of it. During succeeding transactions, relationship rules develop. In a sense, each participant constructs a model of what elements should exist in a relationship. The perspectives deal with rules that "define who can talk to whom, when, where, for how long, or what subject matter, and how" [247]. These relationship rules, whether stated explicitly or not, govern the behavior of the people involved. They prescribe boundaries for acceptable communication behavior in that relationship (Laing [157]). *Both* participants contribute to the formulation of relationship rules. The child who is totally dominated by his father is just as much a party to the role formulation as the father. When the child rebels against the father's definition and begins asserting himself, it becomes clear that the previous model (that he should acquiesce) is what kept the system running smoothly. Whether a relationship is based on symmetry or complementarity, both participants help shape the rules of exchange because they both share the responsibility.

It is assumed in relationships that each one will not only understand the rules, but also observe them. When the rules are violated, it becomes evident just how much reliance is placed on them for a successful relationship. Whenever the rules are either compulsively followed, compulsively disregarded, or changed without informing the partner, it is considered a sign of pathology [246]. For illustrative purposes, consciously break a rule or two in your own transactions. As a student, if you begin assuming control of a class by telling the teacher to raise his hand before speaking and by generally assuming the teacher's role, you can expect a swift reaction. Or in the case of a close friend, for a short period of time engage in disconfirming behavior—ignore him when he talks and change the topic each time you participate. Your friend will likely conclude something is "wrong" with you.

Often the rules agreed upon in one relationship are totally inappropriate in another because, while some rules are generally accepted, others are totally unique to one relationship. For instance, some relationships thrive on one-upmanship, namely, trying to mentally dominate one's partner. Yet when some college debaters try to utilize those rules in their transactions with others, they find the rules inappropriate. One of the author's acquaintances achieves satisfaction by continually complaining about her spouse, both in front of him and when he is not around. I personally have a different set of rules that I prefer to see operate in marital dyads and, as a result, both she and I become uncomfortable when discussing our spouses with each other. Some dyads develop rules that are hard for others to understand, with the destructiveness of the previously mentioned "gruesome twosome" being paramount.

One of the important tasks in analyzing a relationship is to understand what rules are present. Different relationships often demand different rules, and blatant disregard of the rules can bring difficulties into the transaction.

Influencing the Direction of the Relationship.   Understanding the relationship you are in, knowing what function you wish it to serve, and being aware that the rules for it are set forth by you and the other participant are the first steps toward improvement. Often, however, these steps come about only when the relationship has begun to deteriorate. When someone recognizes that the relationship is beginning to run out of control, corrective action is necessary. Relationships have synergy, almost a life of their own, and this momentum has to be pointed to constructive rather than destructive directions.

It was noted in Chapter 4, The Nature of Dyadic Relationships, that all transactions occur on two levels, issue and relationship. Both issue and relationship disagreements involve the mismatching of perspectives and metaperspectives. Issue conflicts, however, are typically more cognitive oriented (what the best solution to a problem is), whereas relationship conflicts focus on the relationship rules. In addition, relationship conflicts are typically more heated and potentially more damaging because they bring doses of disconfirmation with them. A struggle over who has the right to say things is potentially very damaging.

When relational conflicts arise, the relationship tends to build upon itself in the fashion of spirals discussed in Chapter 5. But a spiral can be changed by some techniques available to everyone. If an issue disagreement starts a relational disagreement, then *metacommunicate*. Communicate about your communication [224]. In this "stop the world, I want to get off" device, the participants probe for the relational perspectives and metaperspectives of their partners. Tom and Sam reached the point in a disagreement where Tom said, "Anybody who believes that is a fool," and Sam replied, "You think you're so smart that no one else can contribute anything." It makes no difference who alters the spiral, but he must want to metacommunicate in order to deal with the relational conflict. If in this case Tom were to reply, "What is it I do that gives you the impression that I don't want to listen to your ideas?," the way has been opened for Sam to begin sharing his relational perspectives. The key to altering relational spirals is to break out of the pattern of the "natural" response. If both participants are able to return only hostility to hostility, then those interpersonal "reflexes" will push the relationship so far out of control that it cannot recover. The task is to influence regressive spirals and give them the opportunity to become progessive.

Metacommunication is only one of the possible ways to break the cycle of accusation, defense, and counteraccusation. Instead of seeking to place blame, a participant must accept the situation as given and merely ask himself, "What can I do about it" [247]. Solutions are preferable to accusations. Participants can also stop the transaction and begin again after a "cooling-off period"—a Taft-Hartley injunction for dyadic relationships. And obviously, they can seek the help and counsel of a third party—friend, coworker, or professional counselor.

This "shopping list" of possible ways to improve dyadic relationships, ranging from personal to relationship modifications, consists of only a few select ones. While they are no guarantee of better relationships, these as well as others are worth a try.* We can

---

*It is sometimes impossible for a pair to "work it out" regardless of the ffort expended. The 1974 movie *The Way We Were* provides a provocative account of a romantic dyad that could not work regardless of the best efforts of both participants. The only solace is that on the final parting, they both knew they had tried their best.

often change our relationships for the better by working on them. Human relationships require an investment of time and concern; they do not flourish all by themselves. Life is too short not to enjoy it, and since the "universe is our relations with each other" [104], any improvement in those relations is worth the effort.

SUMMARY

This final chapter offers insight into improving dyadic relationships. Stressing the transactional point of view that each participant's behavior is in part contingent on the other's, it offers some suggestions for dyadic improvement.

One of the most productive and least sought ways to improve your dyadic relationships is to alter your own behavior. If you analyze your needs, identify and change your perceptual sets, and confirm the other person's sense of identity, you can often strengthen a relationship. Changes in your behavior will allow the other person freedom to change, thereby opening the way to relationship improvement.

Awareness of the basic nature of a relationship can also bring improvements. It is important to realize that relationships change and that all relationships require attention. Being aware of the changing nature of a relationship can alert one to potential sources of trouble as the bases of the relationship change over time. In addition, an understanding of the rules of a given relationship can allow one the insight to move the relationship toward a more positive footing. In sum, awareness of the transactional nature of dyadic communicative relationships can give you options to choose from when you want to improve a given relationship.

Appendix
Categories of
Interpersonal Response[*]

1. **Impervious Response.** Speaker fails to acknowledge even minimally the other speaker's communicative attempt. He appears to ignore or disregard the other speaker by making no verbal or nonverbal acknowledgment of his communication.

2. **Interrupting Response.** Speaker begins while the other speaker is still talking; cuts the other speaker off before his point is made. (Does *not* include brief overlaps at end of another's utterance, simultaneous sounds of agreement, as "Yeah," or cases where two persons begin to speak at the same time and one drops out or defers to the other by saying, "Go ahead," or something equivalent.)

3. **Irrelevant Response.** Speaker responds in a way that seems unrelated to what the other speaker has been saying. He may introduce a new topic without warning or may return to his own earlier topic, apparently disregarding the intervening conversation.

4. **Tangential Response.** Speaker acknowledges the other person's communication, but takes the conversation in another direction immediately. This kind of response may take the form of a "tangential shift" or a "tangential drift." The shift is illustrated by the excited child who runs to his mother, saying, "Look at the worm I caught!" and the mother answers, "It's beautiful, now go

*Evelyn Sieburg and Carl Larsen, "Dimensions of Interpersonal Response," paper presented to the International Communication Association Convention, Phoenix, Arizona, April 22–24, 1971.

wash your dirty hands." The drift is illustrated by the speaker who acknowledges the other's communication, but is immediately reminded of something in his own experience and starts to relate it, making a token connection with the other's communication. This category may also include the pseudoresponse, in which the speaker *appears* to be responding to the other speaker because he introduces his own comment with, "Yes, but . . .," "I'm glad you asked that. . .," or gives some other indication that he is going to respond, when in fact he talks about something quite different or unrelated.

5. **Announced Subject Change.** Speaker responds by introducing a new subject, advises the other speaker of his intent to change the subject, or asks permission to change. Examples:

> "Can we go on to something else?"
>
> "I'd like to go back to something we talked about earlier."

6. **Nonverbal Response.** Responder seems attentive and involved in what the other is saying—he smiles, nods, gestures, maintains eye contact with the speaker, or otherwise, expresses interest—but says little or nothing verbally.

7. **Impersonal Response.** Speaker conducts a monologue rather than interacting with the other person. His speech is intellectualized, impersonal, in that it contains few first person statements and more generalized "you" or "one" statements, and may be heavy with euphemisms or cliches. This form of response can be described as being about a subject rather than to a person.

8. **Incoherent Response.** Speaker responds with sentences that are incomplete or with speeches that are rambling, incoherent, or difficult to follow because they contain much retracing, rephrasing, or automisms such as "you know," or "I mean," which add nothing to the content.

9. **Ambiguous Response.** Speaker responds with utterances that contain more than one message or have more than one possible interpretation because of words that are highly abstract or suggestive or private meanings to the speaker. This form of response may negate itself by including both confirmation and

denial in the same utterance, or by "straddling the fence" by saying both yes and no at the same time. (This category refers to verbal ambiguity only.) Examples:

> "I'm not a bit prejudiced, but I'd never want to live next door to a Negro."
>
> "It's none of my business, but it does seem to me . . ."
>
> "I agree with you completely, but . . ." (then explains why he doesn't agree at all)
>
> "Well, it is and it isn't."

10. **Incongruous Response.** Speaker uses nonverbal behavior that does not seem to fit the verbal content. Speaker sends two messages and one seems to deny the other at a different communicative level. Examples:

> "I'm all right—don't worry about me." (said while speaker is weeping)
>
> "Who's angry! I'm not angry!" (said in a tone and volume that strongly suggest anger)
>
> "I'm really concerned about you." (in a tone that suggests anger or irritation)
>
> "Come to mother, dear." (said by a mother to her child in an icy, threatening tone)

11. **Direct Acknowledgment.** Responder acknowledges the other's communication and reacts to it directly and verbally.

12. **Personal Attack.** Responder blames, belittles, expresses contempt for, makes fun of, expresses sarcasm toward, or otherwise disparages the other speaker at a personal level.

13. **Disagreement About Content.** The speaker argues, refutes, denies, or rejects the other speaker's information or opinion. Disagreement is about the subject matter of the other's utterance rather than a personal attack on the other. Examples:

> "I'm sorry, but I just can't go along with that because. . ."
>
> "I think you're wrong about that."

14. **Agreement About Content.**   The speaker reinforces or supports information or opinion expressed by the other speaker. Examples:

> "That's right."
>
> "Yeah" or Uh-huh."
>
> "I read something recently that supports what you say."
>
> "You've really hit on something important there."

15. **Supportive Response.**   The speaker offers the other speaker comfort, expresses understanding of him, protects him, reassures him, takes care of him, or tries to make him feel better. Examples:

> "I know exactly how you feel."
>
> "They've got no right to do that to you!"
>
> "I know you've always done the very best you could."
>
> "With your brains, graduate school will be a snap."

16. **Clarification of Content.**   The speaker tries to clarify the content of another's message. He may elicit more information about the subject, encourage the other to say more about the subject, repeat in a questioning way what the other has just said. Examples:

> "That's not quite clear to me—could you explain it further?"
>
> "Why do you say that?"
>
> "You see yourself as a deeply ambitious person, is that it?"

17. **Clarification of Feelings.**   The speaker tries to clarify the other's present or past feelings. He may elicit further expression of feelings from the other, encourage the other to say more about how he feels, or may repeat the other's words in a questioning way to insure understanding of the feelings expressed. Emphasis here is on *description* of feelings rather than on interpretation or significance of feelings. Examples:

> "Tell me how you're feeling right now."
>
> "You say you are anxious—can you describe further how that feels?"

"Are you trembling, sweating, find it hard to breathe, or what?"

"How did you feel when he said that to you?"

18. **Interpretive Response.** The speaker analyses or asks the other to analyze the significance of what has been said. The speaker may report what he believes to be the other's emotional state, he may deny the other's expressed feelings, or he may insist that the other person really means something other than what he has said. This form of response also includes the pseudopsychiatric diagnosis, in which the responder tells the other what his problem is. Examples:

> "You're not being honest with me."
>
> "You must be very insecure to say something like that."
>
> "I know you don't really mean that."
>
> "I've noticed that you're a very bitter guy."
>
> "What do you suppose is behind this need of yours to have everybody love you?"

19. **Advice About Action.** The speaker tells the other what he ought to do. He directs the other speaker's future behavior, offers suggestions, or presents a plan of action for him. Examples:

> "All right, Joe, I tell you what you gotta do. . ."
>
> "You mustn't act like that."
>
> "What you really need is . . ."
>
> "I'll introduce you to a man who can . . ."

20. **Advice About Feelings.** The speaker tells the other how he ought to feel, or he judges and evaluates the other's expressed feelings. Examples:

> "You shouldn't be hurt—I'm sure she didn't mean anything by it."
>
> "How can you possibly say you're unhappy after all we've done for you!"
>
> "It's downright silly for you to worry about something like that."

"Cheer up! Don't let things get you down."

21. **Expression of Negative Feelings.** The speaker describes his own negative feelings in response to prior utterance of the other. Examples:

> "It makes me feel bad to know you don't trust me."
>
> "That really turns me off!"
>
> "I'm pretty mad about what you just said."

22. **Expression of Positive Feelings.** The speaker describes his own positive feelings in response to prior utterance of the other. Examples:

> "I'm glad you told me that."
>
> "I really like you better for what you just said."
>
> "Okay, now I understand you better."

23. **Helpless Response.** Speaker implies personal inadequacy or uncertainty about himself. Examples:

> "I'm probably wrong, but . . ."
>
> "I shouldn't say this, but . . ."
>
> "I just don't know."
>
> or "I just can't answer that." (used when "I won't answer that," or
>
> "I don't want to answer that" seems more appropriate)

24. **Simple Repetitive Response.** Speaker repeats or closely paraphrases what the other speaker has just said, without questioning, challenging, or interpreting. Examples:

> "You feel you have to be on top no matter what you do to others."
>
> "You've decided you'd do better to make a change."
>
> "You really believe things will be better soon."

References

1. Ackerman, Nathan W., *Psychodynamics of Family Life*. New York: Basic Books, 1958.

2. ———, "Interpersonal Disturbances in the Family: Some Unsolved Problems in Psychotherapy," in *Personality and Social Systems*, Neil J. Smelser and William T. Smelser (eds.). New York: Wiley, 1963, pp. 607–618.

3. ——— (ed.), *Family Therapy in Transition*. Boston: Little, Brown, 1970.

4. Allport, Gordon W., *Pattern and Growth in Personality*. New York: Holt, Rinehart and Winston, 1961.

5. ———, "Is the Concept of Self Necessary?", in *The Self in Social Interaction, Vol. I: Classic and Contemporary Perspectives*, Chad Gordon and Kenneth J. Gergen (eds.). New York: Wiley, 1968, pp. 25–32.

6. Altman, Irwin, and Dalmas A. Taylor, *Social Penetration: The Development of Interpersonal Relationships*. New York: Holt, Rinehart and Winston, 1973.

7. Argyle, Michael, *Social Interaction*. Chicago: Aldine-Atherton, 1969.

8. ———, *The Psychology of Interpersonal Behaviour*. Pelican, 1967.

9. Argyle, Michael, and Marylin Williams, "Observer or Observed? A Reversible Perspective in Person Perception." *Sociometry* 32, No. 4 (December 1969):396–412.

10. Aronson, Elliot, "Some Antecedents of Interpersonal Attraction," in *Nebraska Symposium on Motivation*, Vol. 17, William J. Arnold and David Levine (eds.). Lincoln: University of Nebraska Press, 1969.

11. ———, *The Social Animal*. San Francisco: W. H. Freeman, 1972.

12. Asch, Solomon E., "Forming Impressions of Personality." *Journal of Abnormal and Social Psychology* 41 (1946):258–290.

13. Bach, George R., and Peter Wyden, *The Intimate Enemy*. New York: Avon Books, 1968.

14. Backman, C. W., P. F. Secord, and J. R. Pierce, "Resistance To Change in Self-Concept as a Function of Consensus Among Significant Others." *Sociometry* 25 (1963):102–111.

15. Bales, Robert F., and Edgar F. Borgatta, "Size of Group as a Factor in the Interaction Profile," in A. Paul Hare, *Small Groups: Studies in Social Interaction*, Edgar F. Borgatta, and Robert F. Bales (eds.). New York: Alfred A. Knopf, 1955, pp. 396–413.

16. ———, "Size of Group as a Factor in the Interaction Profile," in A. Paul Hare, *Small Groups: Studies in Social Interaction*, Edgar F. Borgatta and Robert F. Bales (eds.). New York: Alfred A. Knopf, 1965, pp. 495–512.

17. Bardill, Donald R., "A Relationship-Focused Approach to Marital Problems." *Social Work* 11 (July 1966):70–77.

18. Barnlund, Dean C., "Toward a Meaning-Centered Philosophy of Communication." *Journal of Communication* 12 (December 1962):197–211.

19. ———, "A Transactional Model of Communication," in *Foundations of Communication Theory*, Kenneth K. Sereno and C. David Mortensen. New York: Harper and Row, 1970, pp. 83–102.

20. Bateson, Gregory, *Steps to an Ecology of Mind*. New York: Ballantine Books, 1972.

21. Bateson, Gregory, Don D. Jackson, Jay Haley, and John H. Weakland, "Toward a Theory of Schizophrenia." *Behavioral Science* 1, No. 4 (1956):251–264.

22. Beach, Wayne, "Implications of the Dyadic Need for Reciprocity." Paper for Interpersonal Communication 590: Dyadic Communication, March 1974.

23. Bean, Susan S., "Two's Company, Three's a Crowd." *American Anthropologist* 72 (1970):562–564.

24. Becker, Howard, and Ruth Hill Unseem, "Sociological Analysis of the Dyad." *American Sociological Review* 7 No. 1 (1942):13–26.

25. Bennis, Warren G., Edgar H. Schein, Fred I. Steele, and David E. Berlen, *Interpersonal Dynamics*. Homewood, Il: Dorsey Press, 1968.

26. Berger, A. A., "A Test of the Double-Bind Hypothesis of Schizophrenia." *Family Process* 4 (1965):198–205.

27. Berger, Charles A., "Task Performance and Attributional Communication as Determinants of Interpersonal Attraction." *Speech Monographs* 40, No. 4 (November 1973):280–286.

28. Berlo, David, *The Process of Communication*. New York: Holt, Rinehart and Winston, 1960.

29. Berscheid, Ellen, and Elaine Hatfield Walster, *Interpersonal Attraction*. Reading, MA: Addison-Wesley, 1969.

30. Bieri, James, "Changes in Interpersonal Perceptions Following Social Interaction." *Journal of Abnormal and Social Psychology* **48** (1953):61–66.

31. Birdwhistle, Ray, "Contribution of Linguistic-Kinesic Studies to the Understanding of Schizophrenia," in *Schizophrenia: An Integrated Approach*, Alfred Auerback (ed.). New York: Ronald Press, 1959, pp. 99–123.

32. Bleiberg, Aaron H., and Harry E. Leubling, *Parents' Guide to Cleft Palate Rehabilitation*. Jericho, NY: Exposition Press, 1971.

33. Blumberg, Herbert H., "On Being Liked More Than You Like." *Journal of Personality and Social Psychology* **11**, No. 2 (1969):121–128.

34. Blumer, Herbert, "Symbolic Interaction: An Approach to Human Communication," in *Approaches to Human Communication*, Richard W. Budd and Brent D. Ruben. New York: Spartan Books, 1972, pp. 401–419.

35. Bois, J. Samuel, *The Art of Awareness*. Dubuque, IA: William C. Brown, 1973.

36. Bolton, Charles D., "Mate Selection as the Development of a Relationship." *Marriage and Family Living* **23** (August 1961):234–240.

37. Borden, George A., Richard B. Gregg, and Theodore G. Grove, *Speech Behavior and Human Interaction*. Englewood Cliffs, NJ: Prentice-Hall, 1969.

38. Bormann, Ernest G., and Nancy C. Bormann, *Effective Small Group Communication*. Minneapolis: Burgess, 1972.

39. Brewer, Robert E., and Marilynn B. Brewer, "Attraction and Accuracy of Perception in Dyads." *Journal of Personality and Social Psychology* **8**, No. 2 (1968):188–193.

40. Brilhart, John K., *Effective Group Discussion*. Dubuque, IA: William C. Brown, 1967.

41. Bronowski, Jacob, "The Logic of the Mind," in *Man and the Science of Man*, William R. Coulson and Carl R. Rogers. Columbus, OH: Charles E. Merrill, 1968, 31–49.

42. Brown, Charles T., and Paul W. Keller, *Monologue to Dialogue*. Englewood Cliffs, NJ: Prentice-Hall, 1973.

43. Brown, Roger, *Words and Things*. New York: Free Press, 1958.

44. Bruner, Jerome S., David Shapiro, and Renato Tagiuri, "The Meaning

of Traits in Isolation and in Combination," in *Person Perception and Interpersonal Behavior*, Renato Tagiuri and Luigi Petrullo (eds.). Stanford, CA: Stanford University Press, 1958, pp. 277–288.

45. Budd, Richard W., and Brent D. Ruben, *Approaches to Human Communication*. New York: Spartan Books, 1972.

46. Byrne, Donn, "Interpersonal Attraction and Attitude Similarity." *Journal of Social Psychology* 62, No. 3 (1961):713–715.

47. ———, "Attitudes and Attraction," in *Advances in Experimental Social Psychology*, Vol. 4, Leonard Berkowitz (ed.). New York: Academic Press, 1969, pp. 35–89.

48. ———, *The Attraction Paradigm*. New York: Academic Press, 1971.

49. Byrne, Donn, and Barbara Blaylock, "Similarity and Assumed Similarity of Attitudes Between Husbands and Wives." *Journal of Abnormal and Social Psychology* 67, No. 6, (1963):636–640.

50. Cantril, Hadley, *The "Why" of Man's Experience*. New York: Macmillan, 1950.

51. Caplow, Theodore, *Two Against One: Coalitions in Triads*. Englewood Cliffs, NJ: Prentice-Hall, 1968.

51a. Carson, Robert C., *Interaction Concepts of Personality*. Chicago: Aldine, 1969.

52. Chaffee, Steven H., "Pseudo-Data in Communication Research." Paper presented to Communication Theory and Methodology Division, Association for Education in Journalism, Columbia, SC, 1971.

53. Chaffee, Steven H., and Jack M. McLeod, "Sensitization in Panel Design: A Coorientation Experiment." *Journalism Quarterly* 45, No. 4 (Winter 1968):661–669.

54. Chaffee, Steven H., Jack M. McLeod, and Jose L. Guerrero, "Origins and Implications of the Coorientational Approach in Communication Research." Paper presented to the Communication Theory and Methodology Division of the Association for Education in Journalism, Berkeley, CA, 1969.

55. Combs, Arthur W., *The Professional Education of Teachers*. Boston: Allyn and Bacon, 1965.

56. Combs, Arthur W., D. W. Soper, and C. C. Courson, "The Measurement of Self Concept and Self Report." *Educational and Psychological Measurement* 23 (1963):493–500.

57. Cooley, Charles Horton, "The Social Self: On the Meanings of 'I'," in *The Self in Social Interactions, Vol. I: Classic and Contemporary Perspectives*, Chad Gordon and Kenneth J. Gergen (eds.). New York: Wiley, 1968, pp. 87–91.

58. ———, "The Social Self: On the Varities of Self-Feeling," in *The Self in Social Interactions, Vol. I: Classic and Contemporary Perspectives*, Chad Gordon and Kenneth J. Gergen (eds.). New York: Wiley, 1968, pp. 137–143.

59. Coombs, Robert H., "Social Participation, Self-Concept, and Interpersonal Valuation." *Sociometry* **32**, No. 3 (1969):273–286.

60. Costello, Daniel E., "Therapeutic Transactions: An Approach to Human Communication," in *Approaches to Human Communication*, Richard W. Budd and Brent D. Ruben. New York: Spartan Books, 1972, pp. 420–435.

61. ———, "Communication Process: Inclusion of a Space-Time Continuum." Paper presented to International Communication Association, New Orleans, LA, April 1974.

62. Cote, John, "A Conceptualization of Dyads and Triads." Paper for Interpersonal Communication 590: Dyadic Communication, February 1974.

63. Coulson, William R., and Carl R. Rogers, *Man and the Science of Man*. Columbus, OH: Charles E. Merrill, 1968.

64. Cozby, Paul, "Self-Disclosure: A Literature Review." *Psychological Bulletin* **79**, No. 2 (February 1973):73–90.

65. Cronbach, Lee J., "Proposals Leading to Analytic Treatment of Social Perception Scores," in *Person Perception and Interpersonal Behavior*, Renato Tagiuri and Luigi Petrullo (eds.). Stanford, CA: Stanford University Press, 1958, pp. 353–379.

66. Davis, Kingsley E., *Human Society*. New York: Macmillan, 1948.

67. Davis, Kingsley E., and E. E. Jones, "Changes in Interpersonal Perception as a Means of Reducing Cognitive Dissonance." *Journal of Abnormal and Social Psychology* **61** (1960):402–410.

68. DeCharms, Richard, *Personal Causation*. New York: Academic Press, 1968.

69. DeLeon, Patrick H., Jean L. DeLeon, and Phillip J. Swihart, "Relation of Accuracy of Self-Perception and Peer Ratings." *Perceptual and Motor Skills* **29** (1969):966.

70. Delia, Jesse G., Andrew H. Gonyea, and Walter H. Crockett, "Individual Personality Constructs in the Formation of Impressions." Paper presented to Speech Communication Association Convention, Chicago, IL, 1970.

71. Denzin, Norman K., "Rules of Conduct and the Study of Deviant Behavior: Some Notes on Social Relationship," in *Social Relationships*, G. McCall, et al., Aldine-Atherton, 1970, pp. 62–94.

72. DeSaint-Exupery, Antoine, *The Little Prince*. New York: Harcourt, Brace and World, 1943.

73. Dettering, Richard, "The Syntax of Personality." *ETC.: A Review of General Semantics* **26** (June 1969):139–156.

74. DeVries, Egbert, "Explorations in Reciprocity." *Essays on Reciprocity*, Egbert DeVries (ed.). Mouton, 1968, pp. 9–19.

75. —— (ed.), *Essays on Reciprocity*. The Hague: Mouton, 1968.

76. Dewey, John, and Arthur F. Bentley, *Knowing and the Known*. Boston: Beacon Press, 1949.

77. Diggory, James C., *Self-Evaluation: Concepts and Studies*. New York: Wiley, 1966.

78. Drewery, James, "An Interpersonal Perception Technique." *British Journal of Medical Psychology* **42** (1969):171–181.

79. Duck, Steven, *Personal Relationships and Personal Constructs*. New York: Wiley, 1973.

80. Dymond, Rosalind F., "A Scale for the Measurement of Empathic Ability." *Journal of Consulting Psychology* **13** (1949):127–133.

81. Ehrlich, Howard J., and David B. Graeven, "Reciprocal Self-Disclosure in a Dyad." *Journal of Experimental Social Psychology* **7** (1971):389–400.

82. Ellis, Albert, "A Rational Approach to Premarital Counseling." *Psychological Reports* **8** (1961):333–338.

83. ——, "The No Cop-Out Therapy." *Psychology Today*, July 1973, pp. 56–62.

84. Elverud, Kim, "Self Concept." Paper for Interpersonal Communication 590: Dyadic Communication, May 1974.

85. Ericson, Philip M., and L. Edna Rogers, "New Procedures for Analyzing Relational Communication." *Family Process* **12** (1973):245–267.

86. Feffer, Melvin, and Leonard Suchotliff, "Decentering Implications of Social Interactions." *Journal of Personality and Social Psychology* **4**, No. 4 (1966):415–422.

87. Festinger, Leon, "A Theory of Social Comparison Processes." *Human Relations* **2**, No. 2 (May 1954):117–140.

88. Festinger, Leon, S. Schachter, and K. Back, *Social Pressures in Informal Groups: A Study of Human Factors in Housing*. New York: Harper and Row, 1950.

89. Fischer, Paul H., "An Analysis of the Primary Group." *Sociometry* **16** (August 1953):272–276.

90. Frahm, John Harold, "Verbal-Nonverbal Interaction Analysis: Exploring a New Methodology for Quantifying Dyadic Communication Systems." Unpublished dissertation, Michigan State University, 1970.

91. Framo, James L., "Symptoms from a Family Transactional Viewpoint," in *Family Therapy in Transition*, Nathan W. Ackerman (ed.). Boston: Little, Brown, 1970, pp. 125–171.

92. Frank, Frederic, and Lynn R. Anderson, "Effects of Task and Group Size Upon Group Productivity and Member Satisfaction." *Sociometry* **34**, No. 1 (1971):135–149.

93. Frankl, Viktor E., *Man's Search for Meaning: An Introduction to Logotherapy*. New York: Simon and Schuster (Pocket Books), 1972.

94. Franklin, Clyde W., Jr., "Toward a Clarification of Operant Principles in Human Interaction." *The Psychological Record* **20** (1970):489–494.

95. Fromm, Eric, "Selfishness and Self-Love." *Psychiatry* **2** (1939):507–523.

96. ——, *Man For Himself*. New York: Fawcett World Library, 1947.

97. ——, "Selfishness and Self-Love," in *The Self in Social Interaction, Vol. I: Classic and Contemporary Perspectives*, Chad Gordon and Kenneth J. Gergen (eds.). New York: Wiley, pp. 327–337.

98. Garfield, John C., Steven L. Weiss, and Ethan A. Pollack, "Effects of the Child's Social Class on School Counselors' Decision Making." *Journal of Counseling Psychology* **20**, No. 2 (1973):166–168.

99. Gergen, Kenneth J., "Personal Consistency and the Presentation of Self," in *The Self in Social Interaction, Vol. I: Classic and Contemporary Perspectives*, Chad Gordon and Kenneth J. Gergen (eds.). New York: Wiley, 1968, pp. 299–308.

100. ——, *The Concept of Self*. New York: Holt, Rinehart and Winston, 1971.

101. Glass, D. C., "Changes in Liking as a Means of Reducing Cognitive Discrepancies Between Self Esteem and Aggression." *Journal of Personality* **32** (1964): 530–549.

102. Glasser, William, *Reality Therapy*. New York: Harper and Row, 1965.

103. Goffman, Erving, *The Presentation of Self in Everyday Life*. Garden City, NY: Doubleday (Anchor), 1959.

104. Golas, Thaddeus, *The Lazy Man's Guide to Enlightenment*. Palo Alto: The Seed Center, 1971.

105. Gordon, Chad, "Self-Conceptions: Configurations of Content." in

The Self in Social Interaction, Vol. I: Classic and Contemporary Perspectives, Gordon and Gergen (eds.). New York: Wiley, 1968, pp. 115–136.

106.   Gordon, Chad, and Kenneth J. Gergen (eds.), *The Self in Social Interaction, Vol. I: Classic and Contemporary Perspectives.* New York: Wiley, 1968.

107.   Goslin, David A., "Accuracy of Self Perception and Social Acceptance." *Sociometry* 25, No. 3 (Septemer 1962):283–296.

108.   Gouldner, Alvin W., "The Norm of Reciprocity: A Preliminary Statement." *American Sociological Review* 25 (April 1960):161–178.

109.   Gray, Farnum, Paul S. Graubard, and Harry Rosenberg, "Little Brother Is Changing You." *Psychology Today,* March 1974.

110.   Greenburg, Dan, *How To Be A Jewish Mother.* Los Angeles: Price/Stern/Sloan, 1964.

111.   Guthrie, E. R., *The Psychology of Human Conflict.* New York: Harper and Row, 1938.

112.   Haley, Jay, "An Interactional Description of Schizophrenia." *Psychiatry* 22 (1959):321–332.

113.   ———, *Strategies of Psychotherapy.* New York: Grune and Stratton, 1963.

114.   Hamacheck, Don E., *Encounters With The Self.* New York: Holt, Rinehart and Winston, 1971.

115.   Haney, William V., *Communication and Organizational Behavior: Text and Cases,* 3rd ed. Homewood, IL: Richard D. Irwin, 1973.

116.   Hare, A. Paul, *Handbook of Small Group Research.* Glencoe, IL: Free Press, 1965.

117.   Hare, A. Paul, Edgar F. Borgatta, and Robert F. Bales (eds.), *Small Groups.* New York: Alfred A. Knopf, 1966.

118.   Hart, Roderick P., "Perception as a Dependent Variable in Communication: Implications for Research." Paper presented to Speech Communication Association Convention, New York, 1969.

118a. Hastof, Albert H., David J. Schneider, and Judith Polefka, *Person Perception.* Reading, MA: Addison-Wesley, 1970.

119.   Hawkins, Brian, and Cassandra Book, "Relational Communication: An Integration of Theory and Structure." Paper presented to International Communication Association, New Orleans, LA, April 1974.

120.   Hays, William L., "An Approach to the Study of Trait Implication and Trait Similarity." in *Person Perception and Interperson Behavior,*

Renato Tagiuri and Luigi Petrullo. Stanford, CA: Stanford University Press, 1958, pp. 289–299.

121. Heider, Fritz, *The Psychology of Interpersonal Relations*. New York: Wiley, 1958.

122. ——, "Consciousness, the Perceptual World, and Communications with Others." in *Person Perception and Interpersonal Behavior*, Renato Tagiuri and Luigi Petrullo (eds.). Stanford, CA: Stanford University Press, 1958, pp. 22–32.

123. Heine, Patricke Johns, *Personality in Social Theory*. Chicago: Aldine-Atherton, 1971.

124. Heiss, Jerold S., "The Dyad Views the Newcomer." *Human Relations* 16 (1963):241–248.

125. Hendrick, Clyde, "The Study of Interpersonal Attraction." *Acta Symbolica* 2, No. 1 (1971):15–17.

126. Hewitt, Jay, "Liking and the Proportion of Favorable Evaluation." *Journal of Personality and Social Psychology* 22, No. 2 (1972):231–235.

127. Hill, William G., "The Family as a Treatment Unit: Differential Techniques and Procedures." *Social Work* 11 (April 1966):62–68.

128. Hoagland, Hudson, "Science and the New Humanism." *Science* 143 (January 1964):111–114.

129. Hoffman, P. L., L. Festinger, and D. H. Lawrence, "Tendencies Toward Comparability in Competitive Bargaining." *Human Relations* 7 (1954):141–159.

130. Homans, George C., *Social Behavior: Its Elementary Forms*. New York: Harcourt, Brace and World, 1961.

131. Horrocks, John E., and Dorothy W. Jackson, *Self and Role: A Theory of Self-Process and Role Behavior*. Boston: Houghton-Mifflin, 1972.

132. Ichheiser, Gustav, *Appearances and Realities: Misunderstanding in Human Relations*. San Francisco: Jossey-Bass, 1970.

133. Ittelson, William H., and Hadley Cantril, *Perception: A Transactional Approach*. New York: W. W. Norton, 1954.

134. ——, "Perception: A Transactional Approach," in *The Human Dialogue*, Floyd W. Matson and Ashley Montagu. New York: Free Press, 1967, pp. 207–213.

135. Jackson, Don D., "Family Interaction, Family Homeostasis and Some Implications for Conjoint Family Psychotherapy." in *Individual and Familial Dynamics*, Jules H. Masserman (ed.). New York: Grune and Stratton, 1959.

136. James, John, "A Preliminary Study of the Size Determinant in Small Group Interaction." *American Sociological Review* 16, No. 4 (August 1951):474–477.

137. ———, "The Distribution of Free-Forming Small Group Size." *American Sociological Review* 18, No. 15 (October 1953):569–570.

138. James, William, *The Principles of Psychology*, Vol. I. New York: Henry Holt and Company, 1890.

139. ———, "The Self," in *The Self in Social Interaction, Vol. I: Classic and Contemporary Perspectives*, Chad Gordon and Kenneth J. Gergen (eds.). New York: Wiley, 1968, pp. 41–49.

140. Jecker, Jon, and David Landy, "Liking a Person as a Function of Doing Him a Favour." *Human Relations* 22, No. 4 (1969):371–378.

141. Johnson, Wendell, "A Study of the Onset and Development of Stuttering." *Journal of Speech Disorders* 7 (1942):251–257.

142. Johnson, Wendell, and Dorothy Moeller, *Living With Change: The Semantics of Coping*. New York: Harper and Row, 1972.

143. Jones, Edward E., and John Thibaut, "Interaction Goals as Bases of Inference in Interpersonal Perception," in *Person Perception and Interpersonal Behavior*, Renato Tagiuri and Luigi Petrullo (eds.). Stanford, CA: Stanford University Press, 1958, pp. 151–178.

144. Jourard, Sidney, *The Transparent Self*. New York: D. Van Nostrand, 1964.

145. Kelly, George A., *A Theory of Personality: The Psychology of Personal Constructs*, New York: W. W. Norton, 1963.

146. Kendon, Adam, "Some Functions of Gaze-Direction in Social Interaction." *Acta Psychologica* 26 (1967):22–63.

147. Kephart, William M., "A Quantitative Analysis of Intra-Group Relationships." *American Journal of Sociology* 55 (1950):544–549.

148. Kinch, John W., "Experiments on Factors Related to Self-Concept Change." *Journal of Social Psychology* 74 (1968):251–258.

149. ———, "A Formalized Theory of the Self-Concept," in *Symbolic Interaction*, 2nd ed., Jerome Manis and Bernard N. Meltzer (eds.). Boston: Allyn and Bacon, 1972, pp. 245–252.

150. Klemmer, E. T., and F. W. Snyder, "Measurement of Time Spent Communicating." *Journal of Communication* 22 (June 1972):142–158.

151. Krain, Mark, "Communication as a Process of Dyadic Organization and Development." *Journal of Communication* 23 (December 1973):392–408.

152. Kreitman, Norman, "Methods of Measuring Interpersonal Relationships." *Journal of Psychosomatic Research* 10 (1966):109–117.

153. Kurth, Suzanne B., "Friendships and Friendly Relations," in *Social Relationships*, G. McCall, et al., Chicago: Aldine-Atherton, 1970, pp. 136–170.

154. Laing, R. D., *The Divided Self*. Pelican Books, 1960.

155. ———, *The Politics of Experience*. New York: Ballantine Books, 1967.

156. ———, *Self and Others*, 2nd ed. New York: Random House (Pantheon Books), 1969.

157. ———, *The Politics of the Family*. New York: Random House (Vintage), 1969.

158. ———, *Knots,*. New York: Random House (Vintage), 1970.

159. Laing, R. D., and A. Esterson, *Sanity, Madness and the Family*. Baltimore: Pelican Books, 1970.

160. Laing, R. D., H. Phillipson, and A. R. Lee, *Interpersonal Perception*. Baltimore: Perrenial Library, 1966.

161. Lang, Kurt, and Gladys Engel Lang, *Collective Dynamics*. New York: Thomas Y. Crowell, 1961.

162. Leary, Timothy. "The Theory and Measurement Methodology of Interpersonal Communication." *Psychiatry* 18 (May 1955):147–161.

163. Lebra, Takie Sugiyama, "Reciprocity and the Asymmetric Principle: An Analytical Reappraisal of the Japanese Concept of ON." *Psychologia* 12, No. 3 (1969):129–138.

164. Lecky, Prescott, *Self-Consistency: A Theory of Personality*. Fort Myers, FL: Island Press, 1945.

165. Lederer, W. J., and Don D. Jackson, *Mirages of Marriage*. New York: W. W. Norton, 1968.

166. Lennard, Henry L., and Arnold Bernstein, *Patterns in Human Interaction*. San Francisco: Jossey-Bass, 1969.

167. Levinger, George, and James Breedlove, "Interpersonal Attraction and Agreement." *Journal of Personality and Social Psychology* 3, No. 4 (1966):367–372.

168. Lindzey, Gardner, and Elliot Aronson (eds.), *The Handbook of Social Psychology, Vol. I: Historical Introduction*. Reading, MA: Addison-Wesley, 1968.

169. —— (eds.), *The Handbook of Social Psychology, Vol. II: Research Methods*. Reading, MA: Addison-Wesley, 1969.

170. —— (eds.), *The Handbook of Social Psychology, Vol. III: The Individual in a Social Context*. Reading, MA: Addison-Wesley, 1969.

171. Lindzey, Gardner, and Donn Byrne, "Measurement of Social Choice and Interpersonal Attractiveness," in *The Handbook of Social Psychology, Vol. II: Research Methods*, Gardner Lindzey and Elliot Aronson (eds.). Reading, MA: Addison-Wesley, 1969, pp. 452–525.

172. Loeff, R. G., "Differential Discrimination of Conflicting Emotional Messages by Normal, Delinquent, and Schizophrenic Adolescents." University Microfilms No. 66–1470, 1966 (Cited in Schuham, 1967).

173. Lynd, Helen Merrell, "Shame, Guilt, and Identity Beyond Roles," in *The Self in Social Interaction, Vol. I: Classic and Contemporary Perspectives*, Chad Gordon and Kenneth J. Gergen (eds.). New York: Wiley, 1968, pp. 219–226.

174. Manis, Jerome, and Bernard N. Meltzer (eds.), *Symbolic Interaction*, 2nd ed. Boston: Allyn and Bacon, 1972.

175. Mark, Robert A., "Coding Communication at the Relationship Level." *Journal of Communication* 21 (September 1971):221–232.

176. Marlowe, David, and Kenneth J. Gergen, "Personality and Social Interaction," in *The Handbook of Social Psychology, Vol. III: The Individual in a Social Context*, Gardner Lindzey and Elliot Aronson (eds.). Reading, MA: Addison-Wesley, 1969, pp. 590–665.

177. Maslow, Abraham H., "Peak-Experiences as Acute Identity-Experiences," in *The Self in Social Interaction, Vol. I: Classic and Contemporary Perspectives*, Chad Gordon and Kenneth J. Gergen (eds.). New York: Wiley, 1968, pp. 275–280.

178. ——, *Toward a Psychology of Being*. New York: Van Nostrand, 1968.

179. Masserman, Jules H. (ed.), *Individual and Familial Dynamics*. New York: Grune and Stratton, 1959.

180. Matson, Floyd W., and Ashley Montagu, *The Human Dialogue*. New York: Free Press, 1967.

181. May, Rollo, *Man's Search for Himself*. Signet Books, 1953.

182. ——, *Man's Search for Meaning*. Signet Books, 1967.

183. McCall, George J., "The Social Organization of Relationships," in *Social Relationships*, G. McCall, et al. Chicago: Aldine-Atheron, 1970, pp. 3–34.

184. McCall, George J., Michael M. McCall, Norman K. Denyin, Gerald D. Suttles, and Suzanne B. Kurth, *Social Relationships*. Chicago: Aldine-Atherton, 1970.

185. McCall, George J., and J. L. Simmons, *Identities and Interactions*. New York: Free Press, 1966.

186. McCall, Michael M., "Boundary Rules in Relationships and Encounters," in *Social Relationships*, G. McCall, et al. Chicago: Aldine-Atherton, 1970, pp. 35–61.

187. McGuire, Michael T., "Dyadic Communication, Verbal Behavior, Thinking, and Understanding, Vol. I: Background Problems and Theory." *Journal of Nervous and Mental Disease* 152, No. 4 (April 1971):223–241.

188. McGuire, Michael T., and Juliet Stanley, "Dyadic Communication, Verbal Behavior, Thinking, and Understanding, Vol. II: Four Studies." *Journal of Nervous and Mental Disease* 152, No. 4 (April 1971):242–259.

189. McGuire, Michael T., "Dyadic Communication, Verbal Behavior, Thinking, and Understanding, Vol. III: Clinical Observations." *Journal of Nervous and Mental Disease* 152, No. 4 (April 1971):260–277.

190. McGuire, Michael T., and Stephen Torch, "A Model for the Study of Dyadic Communication, Vol. I: Orientation and Model." *Journal of Nervous and Mental Disease* 146, No. 3 (March 1968):221–229.

191. McGuire, Michael T., and Roger Coleman, "A Model for the Study of Dyadic Communication, Vol. II: Research Approach, Research and Discussion." *Journal of Nervous and Mental Disease* 146, No. 3 (March 1968):230–238.

192. McLeod, Jack M., "Issues and Strategies in Coorientational Research." Paper presented to Communication Theory and Methodology Division, Association for Education in Journalism, Columbia, SC, 1971.

193. Mead, George H., *Mind, Self, and Society*, Charles W. Morris (eds.). Chicago: University of Chicago Press, 1934.

194. Meerloo, Joost A. M., *Conversation and Communication*. New York: International Universities Press, 1952.

195. Mehrabian, Albert, *Silent Messages*. Belmont, CA: Wadsworth, 1971.

196. Merton, Robert K., *Social Structure*. New York: Free Press, 1957.

197. Millar, Frank E., III, "A Transactional Analysis of Marital Communication Patterns: An Exploratory Study." Unpublished Ph.D. dissertation, Michigan State University, 1973.

198. Miller, Harold, and Dennis Geller, "Structural Balance in Dyads." *Journal of Personality and Social Psychology* 21, No. 2 (1972):135–138.

199. Mills, Theodore M., "Power Relations in Three-Person Groups." *American Sociological Review* **18** (1953):351–357.

200. Mills, Theodore M., et al., *Group Structure and the Newcomer: An Experimental Study of Group Expansion*. Oslow, Norway: Universitets-forlaget, 1957.

201. Mishler, Elliot, and Nancy E. Waxler, *Interaction in Families*. New York: Wiley, 1968.

202. Miyamoto, S. Frank, and Sanford M. Dornbusch, "A Test of Inter-actionist Hypothesis of Self-Conception." *American Journal of Sociology* **61**, No. 5 (March 1956):399–403.

203. Monge, Peter R. and Richard V. Farace, "Transformations and Message Linkages for a Theory of Communication Orientation." Paper presented to International Communication Association Convention, Atlanta, GA, 1972.

204. Morris, Desmond, *Intimate Behavior*. New York: Bantam Books, 1971.

205. Mortensen, C. David, *Communication: The Study of Human Interaction*. New York: McGraw-Hill, 1972.

206. Murdoch, Peter, "Development of Contractual Norms in a Dyad." *Journal of Personality and Social Psychology* **6** (1967): 206–211.

207. Myers, Gerald E., *Self: An Introduction to Philosophical Psychology*. Indianapolis: Pegasus, 1969.

208. Neuringer, Charles, and Lowell W. Wandke, "Interpersonal Conflicts in Persons of High Self-Concept and Low Self-Concept." *Journal of Social Psychology* **68** (1966):313–322.

209. Newcomb, Theodore M., "An Approach to the Study of Communicative Acts." *Psychological Review* **60** (1953):393–404.

210. ———, *The Acquaintance Process*. New York: Holt, Rinehart, and Winston, 1961.

211. ———, "Stabilities Underlying Changes in Interpersonal Attraction." *Journal of Abnormal and Social Psychology* **66** (1963):376–386.

212. Nierenberg, Gerard I., and Henry Calero, *Meta-Talk*. New York: Trident Press, 1973.

213. Nye, Robert D., *Conflict Among Humans*. New York: Springer, 1973.

214. O'Neill, Nena, and George O'Neill, *Open Marriage*. New York: M. Evans, 1972.

215. ———, *Shifting Gears: Finding Security in a Changing World*. New York: M. Evans, 1974.

216. Parks, Malcolm R., "Towards an Axiomatic Theory of Complementarity and Symmetry." Unpublished paper for Communication 806, Department of Communication, Michigan State University, 1974.

217. ———, "Dyadic Communication From the Perspective of Small Group Research." Paper presented to Central States Speech Association, Milwaukee, WI, 1974.

218. Parks, Malcolm R., William W. Wilmot, and Wesley N. Shellen, "Interpersonal Perception as a Function of Feedback." Unpublished paper, Center for Communication Studies and Services, University of Montana, 1973.

219. Parry, John, *The Psychology of Human Communication*. New York: American Elsevier, 1967.

220. Parsons, Talcott, "Social Structure and the Development of Personality: Freud's Contribution to the Integration of Psychology and Sociology." in *Personality and Social Systems*, Neil J. Smelser and William T. Smelser (eds.). New York: Wiley, 1963, pp. 33–54.

221. Patton, Bobby R., and Kim Giffin, *Interpersonal Communication: Basic Text and Readings*. New York: Harper and Row, 1974.

222. Pearce, W. Barnett, and Stewart M. Sharp, "Self-Disclosing Communication." *Journal of Communication* 23 (December 1973):409–425.

223. Pemberton, William, "Semantics and Communication." *ETC.: A Review of General Semantics* 23 (September 1966):350–353.

224. Pettersen, Duane D., "Communication: A Helping Relationship," Paper presented to International Communication Association, Atlanta, GA, 1972.

225. Piaget, Jean, *The Language and Thought of the Child*. London: Routledge and Kegan Paul, 1926.

226. ———, *Judgment and Reasoning in the Child*. London: Routledge and Kegan Paul, 1928.

227. ———, *The Child's Conception of Physical Causality*. London: Routledge and Kegan Paul, 1930.

228. ———, *The Psychology of Intelligence*. Translated by Malcolm Piercy and D. E. Berlyne, London: Routledge and Kegan Paul, 1950.

229. ———, *Play, Dreams and Imitation in Childhood.* New York: W. W. Norton, 1962.

230. Ralston, Melvin B., and Don Richard Cox, *Emblems of Reality: Discovering Experience in Language*. Beverly Hills, CA: Glencoe Press, 1973.

231. Raush, Harold L., William A. Barry, Richard K. Hertel, and Mary

Ann Swain, *Communication, Conflict and Marriage*. San Francisco: Jossey-Bass, 1974.

232. Riesman, David, *The Lonely Crowd*. New Haven: Yale University Press, 1950.

233. Rogers, Carl R., "Therapy, Personality and Interpersonal Relationships," in *Psychology: A Study of a Science*, Vol. III, S. Koch (ed.). New York: McGraw-Hill, 1959.

234. ———, *Client-Centered Therapy*. Boston: Houghton-Mifflin, 1951.

235. ———, *On Becoming a Person*. Boston: Houghton-Mifflin, 1961.

236. ———, "The Actualizing Tendency in Relation to 'Motives' and to Consciousness," in *Nebraska Symposium on Motivation*, Marshall R. Jones (ed.). Lincoln: University of Nebraska Press, 1963, pp. 1–24.

237. Romey, William D., *Risk-Trust-Love: Learning in a Humane Environment*. Columbus, OH: Charles E. Merrill, 1972.

238. Rosenberg, Morris, "Psychological Selectivity in Self-Esteem Formation," in *Attitude, Ego-Involvement, and Change*, Carolyn W. Sherif and Muzafer Sherif (eds.). New York: Wiley, 1967, pp. 26–50.

239. Rosenthal, Robert, "The Pygmalion Effect Lives." *Psychology Today*, September 1973.

239a. Rosenthal, Robert, and Lenore Jacobson, *Pygmalion in the Classroom*. New York: Holt, Rinehart, and Winston, 1968.

240. Rossiter, Charles M., Jr., "Instruction in Metacommunication." *Central States Speech Journal* 25 (Spring 1974):36–42.

241. ———, "Metacommunication." Paper presented to International Communication Association, New Orleans, LA, April 1974.

242. Ruben, Brent D., "General System Theory: An Approach to Human Communication," in *Approaches to Human Communication*, Richard W. Budd and Brent D. Ruben. New York: Spartan Books, 1972, pp. 120–144.

243. Ruddock, Ralph, *Roles and Relationships*. London: Routledge and Kegan Paul, 1969.

244. Ruesch, Jurgen, "Synopsis of the Theory of Human Communication." *Psychiatry* 16, No. 3 (August 1953):215–243.

245. ———, "Psychiatry and the Challenge of Communication." *Psychiatry* 17, No. 1 (February 1954):1–18.

246. ———, *Disturbed Communication*. New York: W. W. Norton, 1957.

247. ———, *Therapeutic Communication*. New York: W. W. Norton, 1961.

248. Ruesch, Jurgen, and Gregory Bateson, *Communication: The Social Matrix of Psychiatry.* New York: W. W. Norton, 1968.

249. Ruesch, Jurgen, and A. Rodney Prestwood, "Interaction Processes and Personal Codification." *Journal of Personality* 18 (1950):391–430.

250. Ruesch, Jurgen, Jack Block, and Lillian Bennett, "The Assessment of Communication, Vol. I: A Method for the Analysis of Social Interaction." *The Journal of Psychology* 35 (1953):59–80.

251. Rushing, Janice L., and Don G. Rushing, "A Paradigm for Studying Congruence of Perceptions of Communication in a Dyad." Paper presented to International Communication Association, New Orleans, LA, April 1974.

252. Samovar, Larry D., Robert P. Brooks, and Richard Porter, "A Survey of Adult Communication Activities." *Journal of Communication* 19 (December 1969):301–307.

253. Sapolsky, A., "Relationship Between Patient-Doctor Compatibility, Mutual Perception, and Outcome of Treatment." *Journal of Abnormal Psychology* 70 (1965):70–76.

254. Sappenfield, Bert R., "Perceived Similarity to Self as Related to the Stereotypically Perceived 'Ideal Personality'." *Journal of Experimental Research in Personality* 4 (1970):297–302.

255. Sarbin, Theodore R., Ronald Taft, and Daniel E. Bailey, *Clinical Inference and Cognitive Theory.* New York: Holt, Rinehart and Winston, 1960.

256. Sarbin, Theodore R., and Vernon L. Allen, "Role Theory," In *The Handbook of Social Psychology, Vol. I: Historical Introduction*, Gardner Lindzey and Elliot Aronson (eds.). Reading, MA: Addison-Wesley, 1968, pp. 448–567.

257. Schaefer, Early S., "A Circumplex Model for Maternal Behavior." *Journal of Abnormal and Social Psychology* 59 (1959):226–235.

258. Scheff, Thomas J., "Toward a Sociological Model of Consensus." *American Sociological Review* 32 (February 1967):32–46.

259. Scheflen, Albert E., "Regressive One-to-One Relationships." *Psychiatric Quarterly* 34, No. 4 (1960):692–709.

260. ——, *Communicational Structure: Analysis of a Psychotherapy Transaction.* Bloomington, IN: Indiana University Press, 1973.

261. Scheflen, Albert E., and Alice Scheflen, *Body Language and the Social Order.* Englewood Cliffs, NJ: Prentice-Hall, 1972.

262. Schlien, John M., "Phenomenology and Personality," in *Concepts of*

Personality, Joseph W. Wepman and Ralph W. Heine (eds.). Chicago: Aldine-Atherton, 1963, pp. 291–330.

263. Schmuck, Richard A., and Patricia A. Schmuck, *Group Processes in the Classroom.* Dubuque, IA: William C. Brown, 1971.

264. Schopler, John, and John C. Compere, "Effects of Being Kind or Harsh to Another on Liking." *Journal of Personality and Social Psychology* 20, No. 2 (1971):155–159.

264a. Schuham, Anthony I., "The Double-Bind Hypothesis a Decade Later." *Psychological Bulletin* 68, No. 6 (1967):409–416.

265. Schutz, Alfred, *Collected Papers, Vol. I: The Problem of Social Reality,* Maurice Natanson (ed.). Martinus Nijhoff, 1962.

266. ———, *Collected Papers, Vol. II: Studies in Social Theory,* Arvid Brodersen (ed.). Martinus Nijhoff, 1964.

267. Schutz, William C., *The Interpersonal Underworld.* Palo Alto, CA: Science and Behavior Books, 1966.

268. ———, *Joy: Expanding Human Awareness.* New York: Grove Press, 1967.

269. Searles, Harold F., "The Effort to Drive the Other Person Crazy — An Element in the Aetiology and Psychotherapy of Schizophrenia." *The British Journal of Medical Psychology* 32, Pt. 1 (1959):1–18.

270. Sears, Robert R., "A Theoretical Framework for Personality and Social Behavior." *The American Psychologist* 6, No. 9 (September 1951):476–483.

271. Secord, Paul F., and Carl W. Backman, "Personality Theory and the Problem of Stability and Change in Individual Behavior: An Interpersonal Approach." *Psychological Review* 68 (1961):21–33.

272. ———, *Social Psychology.* New York: McGraw-Hill, 1964.

273. Sharp, Stewart M., "A General Systems Approach to the Transactional View of Human Communication." Paper presented to the International Communication Association, New Orleans, LA, April 1974.

274. Shaw, Marvin E., and Philip R. Costanzo, *Theories of Social Psychology.* New York: McGraw-Hill, 1970.

275. Shepherd, Clovis, R., *Small Groups: Some Sociological Perspectives.* San Francisco: Chandler, 1964.

276. Sherif, Carolyn W., and Muzafer Sherif (eds.), *Attitude, Ego-Involvement, and Change.* New York: Wiley, 1967.

277. Shibutani, Tamotsu, *Society and Personality: An Interactionist Approach to Social Psychology.* Englewood Cliffs, NJ: Prentice-Hall, 1961.

277a. Sieburg, Evelyn, and Carl Larson, "Dimensions of Interpersonal Response." Paper presented to International Communication Association Convention, Phoenix, Arizona, April 22–24, 1971.

278. Simmel, Georg, "The Number of Members as Determining the Sociological Form of the Group, I." *American Journal of Sociology* 8, No. 1 (July 1902):1–46.

279. ———, "The Number of Members as Determining the Sociological Form of the Group, II." *American Journal of Sociology* 8, No. 2 (September 1902):158–196.

280. Simon, Walter B., "Helping Transactions: Classificatory and Semantic Considerations." *Psychiatry* 30 (August 1967):249–261.

281. Slater, Philip E., "Contrasting Correlates of Group Size." *Sociometry* 21, No. 2 (June 1958):129–139.

282. Sluzki, Carlos E. and Janet Helmick Beavin, "Simetria y Complementaridad: Una Definicien Operacional y una Tipologia de Parajas." *Acta Psiquiatrica y Psiocologica de America Latina* 11 (1965):321–330.

283. Smelser, Neil J., and William T. Smelser (eds.), *Personality and Social Systems*. New York: Wiley, 1963.

284. ——— (eds.), *Personality and Social Systems*, 2nd ed. New York: Wiley, 1970.

285. Smelser, William T., "Dominance as a Factor in Achievement and Perception in Cooperative Problem Solving Interactions." *Journal of Abnormal Social Psychology* 62 (1961):535–542.

286. Smith, David, "Everyone Talks About Process But No One Does Anything About It." Paper presented to Speech Communication Association Convention, San Francisco, 1971.

287. Smith, J. Rex, "Perception of Self and Other (Mate) as Motivation for Marriage Counseling: An Interactionist Approach." *Sociology and Social Research* 54 (July 1970):466–476.

288. Spiegel, John P., "The Social Roles of Doctor and Patient in Psychoanalysis and Psychotherapy," in *Personality and Social Systems*, Neil J. Smelser and William T. Smelser (eds.). New York: Wiley, 1963, pp. 600–607.

289. Sprott, W. J. H., *Human Groups*. Baltimore: Penguin Books, 1958.

290. Stewart, John (ed.), *Bridges Not Walls*. Reading, MA: Addison-Wesley, 1973.

291. Stone, Gregory P., and Harvey A. Farberman, *Social Psychology Through Symbolic Interaction*. Boston: Ginn, 1970.

292. Streufert, Siegfried, and Susan C. Streufert, "Effects of Conceptual Structure, Failure, and Success on Attribution of Causality and Interpersonal Attitudes." *Journal of Personality and Social Psychology* 11 (1969):138–147.

293. Strodbeck, Fred L., "The Family as a Three-Person Group." *American Sociological Review* 19 (1954):23–29.

294. Suinn, R. M., and J. Geiger, "Stress and the Stability of Self and Other Attitudes." *Journal of General Psychology* 73 (1965):177–180.

295. Sullivan, Harry Stack, *Conceptions of Modern Psychiatry*. New York: W. W. Norton, 1940.

296. ———, *The Interpersonal Theory of Psychiatry*. New York: W. W. Norton, 1953.

297. Suttles, Gerald P., "Friendship as a Social Institution," in *Social Relationships*, G. McCall, et al. Chicago: Aldine-Atherton, 1970, pp. 95–135.

298. Swensen, Clifford H., Jr., *Introduction to Interpersonal Relations*. Glenview, IL: Scott Foresman, 1973.

299. Tagiuri, Renato, "Relational Analysis: An Extension of Sociometric Method with Emphasis Upon Social Perception." *Sociometry* 15, Nos. 1–2 (February–May 1952):91–104.

300. ———, "Social Preference and Its Perception," in *Person Perception and Interpersonal Behavior*, Renato Tagiuri and Luigi Petrullo (eds.). Stanford, CA: Stanford University Press, 1958, pp. 316–336.

301. ———, "Person Perception," in *The Handbook of Social Psychology, Vol. III: The Individual in a Social Context*, Gardner Lindzey and Elliot Aronson (eds.). Reading, MA: Addison-Wesley, 1969, pp. 395–449.

302. Tagiuri, Renato, Jerome S. Bruner, and Robert R. Blake, "On the Relation Between Feelings and Perception of Feelings Among Members of Small Groups," in *Readings in Social Psychology*, 3rd ed., Eleanor Maccoby, Theodore M. Newcomb, and Eugene L. Hartley (eds.). New York: Holt, Rinehart and Winston, 1958, pp. 110–116.

303. Tagiuri, Renato, and Luigi Petrullo (eds.), *Person Perception and Interpersonal Behavior*. Stanford, CA: Stanford University Press, 1958.

304. Taylor, F. Kraupl, "Awareness of One's Social Appeal." *Human Relations* 9, No. 1 (1956):47–56.

305. ———, "Display of Dyadic Emotions." *Human Relations* 10, No. 3 (1957):257–262.

306. Taylor, Howard F., *Balance in Small Groups*. New York: Van Nostrand, 1970.

307. Thibaut, John W., and Harold H. Kelley, *The Social Psychology of Groups*. New York: Wiley, 1959.

308. Thomas, Edwin J., and Clinton F. Fink, "Effects of Group Size," in *Small Groups: Studies in Social Interaction*, A. Paul Hare, Edgar F. Borgatta, and Robert F. Bales (eds.). New York: Alfred A. Knopf, 1966, pp. 525–536.

309. Thomas, William I., and Dorothy Swaine Thomas, *The Child in America*. New York: Alfred A. Knopf, 1928.

310. Tipton, Leonard P., "Agreement and Accuracy in Dyadic Communication." Paper presented to International Communication Association, Phoenix, AZ, 1971.

311. Tiryakian, Edward A., "The Existential Self and the Person," in *The Self in Social Interaction, Vol. I: Classic and Contemporary Perspectives*, Chad Gordon and Kenneth J. Gergen (eds.). New York: Wiley, 1968, pp. 75–86.

312. Toch, Hans, and Henry Clay Smith (eds.), *Social Perception*. New York: Van Nostrand, 1968.

313. Triandis, Harry C., "Cognitive Similarity and Communication in a Dyad." *Human Relations* 13, No. 2 (1960):175–183.

314. ——, "Some Determinants of Interpersonal Communication." *Human Relations* 13, No. 3 (August 1960):279–287.

315. Turney-High, Harry Holbert, *Man and System: Foundations for the Study of Human Relations*. New York: Appleton-Century-Crofts, 1968.

316. Van Peursen, C. A., "Notes for a Philosophy of Reciprocity," in *Essays on Reciprocity*, Egbert DeVries (ed.). The Hague: Mouton, 1968, 20–39.

317. Varela, Jacobo A., *Psychological Solutions to Social Problems*. New York: Academic Press, 1971.

318. Vernon, Glen M., *Human Interaction: An Introduction to Sociology*, 2nd ed. New York: Ronald Press, 1972.

319. Vernon, M. D., *The Psychology of Perception*. Baltimore: Penguin Books, 1962.

320. Von Wiese, Leopold, *Systematic Sociology*. Translated by Howard Becker. New York: Wiley, 1932.

321. Wackman, Daniel, B., "A Proposal for a New Measure of Coorientational Accuracy or Empathy." Paper presented to the Communication Theory and Methodology Division of the Association for Education in Journalism, Berkeley, CA, August 1969.

322. ———, "Interpersonal Communication and Coorientation." Paper presented to the Communication Theory and Methodology Division of the Association for Education in Journalism, Columbia, SC, August 1971.

323. Waller, Willard, and Reuben Hill, *The Family: A Dynamic Interpretation.* Hinsdale, IL: Dryden Press, 1951.

324. Walster, Elaine, "The Effect of Self-Esteem on Liking for Dates of Various Social Desirabilities." *Journal of Experimental Social Psychology* 6 (1970): 248–253.

325. Walster, Elaine, Vera Aronson, Darcy Abrahams, and Leon Rottman, "Importance of Physical Attractiveness in Dating Behavior." *Journal of Personality and Social Psychology* 4, No. 5 (1966):508–516.

326. Warr, Peter B., and Christopher Knapper, *The Perception of People and Events.* New York: Wiley, 1968.

327. Watson, Jeanne, and Robert J. Potter, "An Analytic Unit for the Study of Interaction," *Human Relations* 15, No. 3 (August 1962):245–263.

328. Watts, Alan W., *Psychotheraphy East and West.* New York: Ballantine Books, 1961.

329. Watzlawick, Paul, and Janet Helmick Beavin, "Some Formal Aspects of Communication." *American Behavioral Scientist 10*, No. 8 (April 1967):4–8.

330. Watzlawick, Paul, Janet Helmick Beavin, and Don D. Jackson, *The Pragmatics of Human Communication.* New York: W. W. Norton, 1967.

331. Weakland, John H., "Communication and Behavior — An Introduction." *American Behavioral Scientist 10*, No. 8 (April 1967):1–4.

332. Weisskopf-Joelson, Edith, "Some Comments on a Viennese School of Psychiatry." *The Journal of Abnormal and Social Psychology* 51 (1955):701–703.

333. Wenburg, John R., John A. Boyd, and Benjamin Whitney Morse VI, "Dyadic Relationships: How Credibility Functions." Paper presented at Central States Speech Association Convention, Milwaukee, WI, April 1974.

334. Wenburg, John R., and William W. Wilmot, *The Personal Communication Process.* New York: Wiley, 1973.

335. Wender, Paul H., "Communicative Unclarity: Some Comments on the Rhetoric of Confusion." *Psychiatry* 30 (1967):332–349.

336. Wepman, Joseph M., and Ralph W. Heine, *Concepts of Personality.* Chicago: Aldine-Atherton, 1963.

337. Wheeler, Ladd, *Interpersonal Influence.* Boston: Allyn and Bacon, 1970.

338. Whyte, William H., Jr., *The Organization Man*. Garden City, NY: Doubleday (Anchor), 1957.

339. Wiener, Daniel J., "Failure of Personality Variables to Mediate Interpersonal Attraction." *Psychological Reports* **26** (1970):784–786.

340. Will, Otto, "Human Relations and the Schizophrenia Reaction." *Psychiatry* **22** (1959):205–223.

341. Wilmot, William W., and John R. Wenburg, "Communication as Transaction." Paper presented to International Communication Association, Montreal, Canada, 1973.

342. ———, *Communication Involvement: Personal Perspectives*. New York: Wiley, 1974.

343. Wolff, Kurt H. (ed. and Trans.), *The Sociology of Georg Simmel*. New York: Free Press, 1950.

344. Woodman, Loring, *Perspectives in Self-Awareness: Essays on Human Problems*. Columbus, OH: Charles E. Merrill, 1973.

345. Word, Carl O., Mark P. Zanna, and Joel Cooper, "The Nonverbal Mediation of Self-Fulfilling Prophecies in Interracial Interactions." *Journal of Experimental Social Psychology* **10** (1974):109–120.

346. Worthy, Morgan, Albert C. Gary, and Gay M. Kahn, "Self-Disclosure as an Exchange Process." *Journal of Personality and Social Psychology* **13**, No. 1 (1969):59–63.

347. Wylie, Ruth C., *The Self-Concept: A Critical Survey of Pertinent Research Literature*. Lincoln: University of Nebraska Press, 1961.

348. ———, *The Self-Concept: A Review of Methodological Considerations and Measuring Instruments*, Vol. I, revised edition. Lincoln: University of Nebraska Press, 1974.

349. Yablonsky, Lewis, "The Sociometry of the Dyad." *Sociometry* **18** (1955):613–616.

349a. Ziller, Robert C., *The Social Self*. New York: Pergamon Press, 1973.

350. Zimbardo, Philip, "The Pathology of Imprisonment." *Society* **9**, No. 6 (1972):4–8.

351. Zimet, Carl N., and Carol Schneider, "Effects of Group Size on Interaction in Small Groups." *Journal of Social Psychology* **77** (1969):177–187.

Index

Index

Allport, G., 66
Altman I., and D. A. Taylor, 66, 153
Appearances and reality, 33
Asch, S., 62
Attributing causality, 64
Attribution theory, 65

Balance theory, 72
Bales, R. F., and E. F. Borgatta, 15
Beach, W., 34
Behavior, influence on perception, 73
Bennis, W., 154
Bleiberg, A., 43

Caplow, T., 22
Carson, R., 103
Chaffee, S. H., and J. M. McLeod, 86, 87
Circularity, 82
Circumplex, 104
Click, J., 129
Conflict, 15
    issue, 99
    relationship, 99
Congruence, 50
Cooley, J., 41, 54
Coombs, R., 47
Coorientation, 84

Communication, assumptions of, 6
    defined, 6
Completeness of dyads, 16
Counselor (third party), 24
Cyclic processes, 74

Definition of relationship, 108
Disconfirmation, 151
Distinctiveness of dyads, 18
Do-loops, 135
Dominance/submission, 103
Double-bind, 132
Drewery, J., 88
Duck, S., 72
Dyad, distinctiveness of, 18
    strengthening it, 24
    as a unit, 7
Dyadic effect, 124, 153
Dyadic characteristics, 12
Dyadic coalitions, 22, 27
    permanency of, 28
    prediction of, 29
Dyadic communication, classi-
    fied, 5
    defined, 4
    frequency, 12
Dyadic improvements, 143
Dymond, 3

Equifinality, 82
Escher, M. C., 21
Expectation of consistency, 63

Feedback needs, 15
Festinger, L., 48, 69
Fischer, P., 12
Frankl, V., 42, 136
"Frogs and Princes," 53

Garfield, J., 121
Gergen, K., 42
Goffman, E., 49, 103
Golas, T., 132
Gordon, C., 42
Glass, D., 73
Group size, 19
Gruesome twosome, 126
Guthrie, E., 43

Hamachek, D., 52
Haney, W., 150
Hare, A., 19
Hastorf, A., 65, 74
Heine, P., 45
Hendrick, C., 73

Influence, mutual effects, 10
Interpersonal perception method, 88
Interpersonal attraction, 68
Intimacy, consequences of, 14
    dyadic communication, 13
"I see you seeing me," 81
Issues, 96

Jackson, D., 103
James, W., 38, 48, 49
Johnson, W., 117
Jones, E. E., and J. Thibaut, 111

Kelly, G., 63
Kinch, J., 43, 46
Kurth, S., 103

Laing, R. D., 42, 45, 88, 137
Leary, T., 104
Lederer, W. J., and D. D. Jackson,
    152
Levinger, G., 72
Love/hate, 103

Majority opinion, 17
May, R., 39
McCall, G., 103
McGuire, W., 147
Merton, R., 117
Metacommunicate, 158
Mother-in-law, 26
Multiple relationships, 19
Mutually shared field, 61

Needs, self-analysis of, 144
Negotiation, social identities, 94
Newcomb, T., 70

Other, confirmation of the, 150
    expectations of the, 50

Paradoxes, 130
    double-bind, 132
"People have reasons," 149
Perception, accuracy of, 65
    checking, 145
    identifying, 146
    of objects, 60
    of being perceived, 81
    seeking others', 148
    transactional, 59
Perceptual accuracy, 67
Perls, F., 50
Person perception, mutually shared
    field, 61
    principles, 62
    regularities, 62
    transactional, 59, 74
Personal constructs, 63

Perspectives, comparison of, 84
    direct, 89
    meta, 89
    meta-meta, 89
Potential relationships, 19
Propinquity, 68

Real self, 51
Real you, 37
Reciprocal ignorance, 3
Reciprocity, 110
    types of, 111
Regressiveness, 135
Relational conflict, 101
Relationships, analysis of, 84, 152
    changing direction of, 157
    complementary, 106
    denying existence of, 102
    dimensions of, 103
    elements of, 81
    good, 154
    parallel, 106
    rules of, 156
    symmetrical, 106
    types of, 154
Rogers, C., 50
Rosenberg, M., 52, 67
Rosenthal, R., 43, 120
Ruesch, J., 42, 103, 147, 150

Sarbin, T., 50, 111
Schizophrenia, 133
Selective interpretation, 52
Selective exposure, 53
Selectivity, self-concept, 52
Self, looking-glass, 42
    material, 38
    social, 38, 41
Self-awareness, 35
Self-concept, change, 51
    components, 35

cyclic process, 45
    defined, 34
    maintenance, 51
Self-esteem, 41
Self-fulfilling prophecies, 117
    utilizing, 122
Self-reflexiveness, 34
    disruption and, 35
    do-loops, 136
Selves, multiple, 37
Similarity, 71
Simmel, G., 25
Social comparison, 47
Social roles, 49
Social system increases 18, 19
Spirals, 122
    alternating, 127
    progressive, 124
    regressive, 126
Stewart, J., 42
Sullivan, H., 42
Synergy, 82
System, communication, 82

Tagiuri, R., 61, 93
Tangential response, 151
Third person, and dyad, 24, 25
Thomas, W., 117
Tiryakian, E., 42
Transactional assumptions, 11
Transactional nature, 8
Transactional pattern of relations, 84
Triad, functional view, 21
    innate instability, 23
    united feeling, 21

Variables, cause-effect, 46
    independent-dependent, 11
Vinacke-Ackoff, 28
Von Wiese, L., 4, 12, 17

Wallace, S., 53
Wenburg, J., 62, 96, 111, 151
Wholeness, 82
Wilmot, W., 96, 111, 151
Woodman, L., 42, 44, 135, 136,
    137

Yablonsky, L., 103

Zimbardo, P., 127